Pawnbroker's Handbook

v. Alexander Cullen

How to Get Rich

Buying and

Selling Guns,

Gold, and Other

Good Stuff

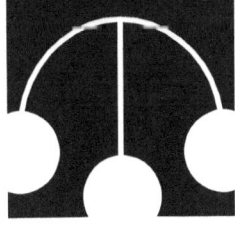

Pawnbroker's Handbook:
How to Get Rich Buying and Selling Guns, Gold, and Other Good Stuff
by V. Alexander Cullen

Printed in the United States of America

Contents

1 A Short History of Pawnbrokers

Pawnshops date back to ancient history and were one of the first lending institutions. Pawnbroking is one of the oldest trades known to man and is often called the "world's second oldest profession." The trade of pawnbroking is first mentioned in the Old Testament in Exodus 22. It can be traced back more than 3,000 years in China and can also be found in written histories of the Greek and Roman civilizations. These ancient pawnbrokers were responsible for laying many of the legal foundations upon which many of our modern regulations in banking and finance are built.

During the Middle Ages, certain usury laws imposed by the Roman Catholic Church prohibited the charging of interest on loans, thus limiting pawnbroking to people whose religious beliefs did not conflict with the Church. Many pawnshops came into being because of problems in the banking system. During this time, the Lombards of northern Italy operated pawnshops throughout Europe, counting royalty among their clientele (King Edward III of England was a customer of the Lombards).

The three gold balls that symbolize pawnshops are derived from the ones used by the Lombards and can be traced to the coat of arms of the Medici family of Florence, Italy. The Medici bankers lent money in exchange for farming equipment during the off season. To this day, the three balls remain as the universal symbol of pawnbroking.

Pawnbroking first played a part in the development of America when Christopher Columbus asked Queen Isabella of Spain to finance his first voyage to the then unknown New World. She was prepared to pawn her crown jewels to help him finance the venture, but then King Ferdinand agreed to back Columbus, thereby saving the Queen from having to part with her jewels. America's first settlers brought pawnbroking with them, and it was often their only source of finances. As the country grew, the demand for credit did also. Financial institutions such as banks, consumer and commercial finance companies, and savings and loan companies sprang into business. Many of these firms can trace their origins to these first pawnbrokers.

In the United States, as in most parts of the world, pawnshops are usually small "mom-and-pop" type businesses licensed and regulated by national, state, county, or city governments. In contrast, though, are large pawnbroking corporations like Cash America, which has more than 250 stores worldwide and revenues of more than $185 million. The large pawnshops issue stock, which is traded on the New York Stock Exchange.

What's in the future for pawnbroking in this country? I believe the outlook is unlimited, and anyone with money to invest and a willingness to work hard can be a success. Every town across America should have at least one pawnshop.

ALEXANDER'S PAWNSHOP

My story begins in 1979. After spending three years working my way to a supervisor's position in a local foundry, I decided to leave the mechanized meaninglessness of assembly-line work to become an employee in my father's pawnshop. I worked in this capacity for five years, steadily acquiring the knowledge, skills, and business acumen that I would eventually need to succeed on my own. I attended a six-month course for jewelry repair in Lancaster, Pennsylvania, at Bowman's School. In 1984, with my father's blessing, I received a $30,000 loan and started my own pawnshop. In the nine years since taking this step, I've made more than $300,000 in profit and held up to $40,000 in small loans that legally earn 120 percent interest per year. I now own a small business that is valued at more than $200,000, and I bought the shopping center in which I originally rented space, which has allowed me to double the size of my original store while leaving enough rental space to pay my mortgage every month so that my store space is rent free.

On a more personal note, I've retired the mortgage on my old home and bought a new 3,400-square-foot house near my business. It's worth over $250,000 and has an acre of land and an in-ground pool. I own two late model automobiles, take several worry-free vacations every year, donate generously to my favorite charities, and, best of all, I work a comfortable 45-hour week in an environment where I am my own boss. I also have the personal satisfaction of knowing that my family's future is financially sound, and my children will have the opportunity to attend the college or technical school of their choice.

If you are a collector like I am, you may appreciate the fact that I am able to buy coins, stamps, guns, and jewelry at ridiculously low prices. Furthermore, I don't have to search for these treasures; they come to me every day of the week right in the comfort of my own store. Besides collectibles, my pawnshop has also provided me with every stereo system, television, musical instrument, camera, and tool that I've ever wanted. I can also give generous gifts of merchandise to my friends and family for birthdays and Christmas. For example, I was able to give my wife a Rolex watch for Christmas this year that retails new for $4,200. I was able to buy it for only $800.

Last, but not least, my business affords me the fulfillment and satisfaction of helping people in need. A person can come to me and instantly obtain the cash they require to meet their financial obligations simply by pledging a suitable piece of collateral. In my opinion, being able to assist people in this way provides twice the profit for the money, making a pawnshop one of the best investments in the world.

If you are wondering about the stability and security of such a business venture in the face of an uncertain economic future, let me tell you that my faith in pawnshops is well supported both by my personal experience and by recorded history. My family's pawnshop thrived in the late 1970s and 1980s when most of the rest of the country was in the throes of a recession. In addition, when you consider that a pawn is the oldest form of loan agreement known to man, and that pawnbrokers have survived economic chaos and turmoil since biblical times, it simply stands to reason that they are one of the safest businesses imaginable.

I plan to continue operating my pawnshop for the rest of my life. As I get older, I may work part time and have my sons or other family members take over the full-time management of the business. My father is still operating his pawnshop and works part-time while preparing one of his grandchildren to take over the business. He was a career army officer and a decorated veteran of three wars. He retired as a lieutenant colonel and purchased his pawnshop from an old pawnbroking family in 1974. In the last 19 years, he has become a millionaire. He lives in a waterfront estate worth more than half a million dollars and enjoys an active, fulfilled retirement.

My point in sharing all of this is that I can teach anyone to duplicate or surpass our achievements. All that's required is working capital and a desire to succeed. The risk of failure is actually quite low since the majority of your funds will be invested in quality loan collateral. Using my methods, a pawnbroker can establish a business by working 40 to 50 hours per week. My experience and knowledge will save you thousands of dollars in mistakes.

2 Where to Put Your Pawnshop

Someone once said the three most important things for a successful business is location, location, and location. Indeed, this can be the most important decision you make in determining the success or failure of your venture into the pawnshop business. Things to consider when looking for a location for your pawnshop include: zoning restrictions, local law enforcement, retail traffic, price, size, and space.

ZONING RESTRICTIONS

Before you can even begin your search for store space, you must find out where you will be allowed by the local government to operate your pawnshop. Some areas are very lax and have no laws zoning pawnshops, while other localities are very restrictive, even regulating how many pawnshops may be located in any given area. I have been to cities where pawnshops can operate freely, like other retail businesses, in any part of town where they can find space, even in large shopping malls. Other towns have attempted to zone pawnshops completely out or restrict them to areas considered to be bad neighborhoods.

I once tried to move my pawnshop less than two miles down the road, and even though I had been in business several years with no adverse effect to the local community, they initially reacted like I wanted to put in a nuclear waste dump. After I opened the first pawnshop in the county in 1984, the zoning board discovered they had no ordinance to cover pawnshops, so they immediately wrote a rather restrictive one. They included other undesirable businesses like tattoo parlors and palm readers in it also. I found it necessary to hire a consultant (who had once been a member of the board) and paid him to grease the wheels of progress, so to speak. I finally won approval for the move after four months of planning commissions and board of supervisors meetings. (I ended up staying put when I was able to buy my shopping center.)

You will need to find out about all zoning requirements from your local board before you commit to any leases or other contracts for space.

GETTING YOUR PAWNBROKER'S LICENSE

When my father and I first came to York County to look for a place to open my shop, we consulted with the local sheriff, informed him of our intentions, and won his approval so we could get our business license. This is the next thing you should do after going to the zoning board.

You should have a good working relationship with the chief law enforcement officer in charge of the locality where you plan to open your pawnshop. He will run a thorough background check on you. Any thing improper (felonies mainly) can disqualify you from holding a pawnbroker's license, not to mention the federal and/or state firearms licenses you will need in order to pawn and dispose of firearms. This local law enforcement agency will also be the one that reviews your pawn sheets for stolen property. Many times their judgment means the difference between your keeping an item or losing it.

TYPE OF SPACE

Once you've discovered what area of your city or county is zoned for pawnshops and you are given approval to get your license, you can start looking for a space. When I first opened my pawnshop in 1984, my father and I looked at both stand-alone and shopping center spaces. Both have advantages and disadvantages.

First you must consider whether the landlord, neighbors, and other tenants will welcome you. Part of the reason the county resisted the relocation of my pawnshop was that a new school was to be built within a block of that location.

Also consider that other merchants who sell jewelry, guns, musical instruments, electronics, etc., may not like competition from a pawnshop. I was lucky that I found the small shopping center space I have now, because none of the other merchants in the center at that time objected to my pawnshop. This is something you must consider for your own benefit as well, because a gun store or jeweler next door will burden your new pawn-shop with competition you don't need.

Other neighbors to avoid are other pawnshops, secondhand stores, flea markets, and any other business that buys used merchandise. Your customers are just like you—they want the "mostest for the leastest." If presented with the opportunity, most people will ride up and down the road or walk across the street or, even worse, right next door to conduct an auction for their merchandise.

SECURITY AND RETAIL TRAFFIC

An advantage of being in a small shopping center like mine is it gives you more security. In my shopping center, there is a 7-11 on one end that is open 24 hours and a take-out Pizza Hut in the middle that stays open till one or two o'clock in the morning. These businesses keep people coming and going at all hours, thereby discouraging thieves and also giving me greater exposure to more potential customers.

This shopping center is situated in an area that has access to three major highways and an interstate highway. This gives me access to a population of more than 1 million in the Tidewater area of Virginia, even though I'm in the rural suburb of York County. I have customers that will drive 50 or 60 miles to do business with me because I'm easily accessible by these highways. It's been my experience that people will seek you out when you have money to offer for loans or purchases and you are easy to get to.

AMOUNT OF SPACE AND PRICE

The amount of space and price should also be considered when choosing a place to start your pawnshop. I started with 1,500 square feet in 1984, which cost me $600 per month. There were also other charges for common area maintenance, water, and sewer, which amounted to another $100 per month. I was able to expand into the space next door, giving me a total of 3,000 square feet, when I bought the shopping center and had enough tenants to cover the mortgage payment so my space was rent free. Most of my tenants pay an average of 50¢ per square foot per month, but other shopping centers charge $1 to $2 per square foot per month and higher.

I recommend that you start with at least 1,200 square feet but less than 2,000 square feet, unless you get a real bargain price. With too little space, you could grow out of it too fast. With too much space, your overhead could be more than your new business can handle. The larger your space, the larger your rent, utilities, taxes, etc. High overhead has killed a lot of new businesses that otherwise would have made it. At the same time, you will need enough space to be comfortable. You will be spending a large portion of your life in this place, as much as 50 or 60 hours per week 50 weeks per year in the beginning.

MERCHANDISE AND STORAGE

You must also consider what kind of merchandise you will be taking in pawn. Some pawnbrokers take in large items that must be stored indoors, like compressors, generators, motorcycles, and large toolboxes. What about cars, boats, campers, and motorhomes? They need a secure, fenced-in area for proper storage.

When you loan people money on their valuable property, you must make every effort to keep it dry, secure, and in good condition for their benefit as well as yours. People will hold you responsible for damage done to their goods.

(Above) Always have space to store large items in pawn, like rolling toolboxes, tall speakers, and air compressors.

(Left) Large items in pawn, like guitars and televisions, can be stored on homemade shelves like these.

Commercial shelves like these are good for storing flat items in pawn, like videocassette recorders (VCRs) and stereo components.

I built this rack to store long guns that are in pawn.

This storage box holds most of my "in pawn" jewelry. I attach computer-generated tags with pawn ticket numbers to the 3 1/2-by-6 1/2-inch coin bags and file them in numerical order.

LICENSES

Every state and local jurisdiction requires different licenses. My area requires a general business license and a zoning permit for pawnshops. There is also a seperate license for buying gold. When you apply for your license to operate a pawnshop, obtain a copy of all the state laws governing your business. I have included a copy of the Virginia laws in Appendix A.

Always acquire the proper licenses, and follow the letter of the law to keep them. And don't delay in applying for them, because it may take months to get them. As I said earlier, the local constabulary will be checking your store on a regular basis, and anything you do without a proper license may result in your prosecution.

3 Security

The next thing you need to consider even before you put in your first showcase or piece of merchandise is security. Security, in my opinion, is second in importance only to the legal licensing and location of your pawnshop. Your business will be a prime target for thieves, but with a good plan for security, you can be 99-percent safe.

WINDOWS

When I finally got my license and rented my store space, the very first thing I did was put iron bars on the windows. The building had three 8-by-3-foot glass windows and a glass door with a window above it. It is essential to bar or cover all glass that can be smashed to gain illegal entry. Every vent, skylight, and window that a skinny thief can wiggle through should also be covered.

When my father first started his pawnshop in 1975, he had two doors in front of his shop that were made of 2-inch-thick glass. These doors had hung in this doorway for more than 40 years. Even though he put security screen over all the windows and vents, thieves still smashed one of the doors (it took several blows with a 12-pound cinder block) and carried away more than $3,000 worth of hand-guns. (Of 20 handguns taken, only two have been recovered in the last 19 years.) After this incident, he installed a pull-down security grate.

This was the type of thing I wished to install when I first opened my shop in 1984, but the landlord did not like the idea. He insisted that any security bars be installed on the inside. So I went to the local iron monger and bought bar stock from which I cut lengths with a hacksaw. I then drew a diagram of how I wanted them assembled and had them welded together. With a coat of paint, the finished product looked as good as anything a pro could build, and it cost me

These homemade security bars will stop most smash-and-grabbers.

A front view of my security bars.

hundreds less. I mounted these bars to the metal frame of the windows with heavy-duty sheet metal screws. The result was a clean and strong professional security system that has not failed me yet.

If you have any windows in your future pawnshop, security screen or iron bars are the only defense against what I call the "smash-and-grab" robbery. A smash-and-grab robbery is one where a thief smashes through a window or door, grabs as much of your property as he can carry, then hauls ass before you or the local constabulary can arrive to catch him. It's kind of like looting, only it's not done by a rioting mob. Even though the thief knows that he will set off your alarm system (alarm systems are covered later), he also knows that he will have several minutes to escape with the loot.

DOORS

Door locks and hinges should also be considered when beefing up security. Both of my back doors are made of heavy steel and are mounted in steel frames. I have dead-bolt locks on both, and one has an old jailhouse door mounted on the inside also.

The one door I come and go through had only a dead bolt and locking door knob, which I used to consider enough. Just before Christmas this year, a thief attempted to break into my pawnshop through this door. He took a large crowbar and pried the door open by bending the door and the frame. Once inside my office, he tripped the alarm and was confronted by a second locked door, which separates my office from the main sales area of the shop. Also, there is a video monitor in my office for one of the surveillance cameras in the sales area. The thief may have noticed the monitor and realized that the camera would show him entering the sales area. This is what I like to call a layered defense system. The harder you make it for thieves and the more layers of security they have to penetrate, the better for you and the security of your business. After all, people steal because they don't want to work hard. Layers of security can slow down a thief long enough so that the risk of being caught increases.

After this incident, I had a locksmith install a device that prevents a prybar from being inserted in the space between the door and the frame. (I plan to have pins installed to keep a thief from taking this door off its hinges as well.) I also had the locksmith install rings on the dead-bolt locks on my front doors. These prevent a thief from using a pipe

This second entrance door gets extra security with bolt-cutter-proof locks on a steel hasp.

wrench or channel locks to break the locks open. I keep one of my front doors locked all the time with not just the dead bolt but three metal hasp and bolt-cutter-proof locks.

The best thing to do when you first open is have your local locksmith check all your locks, doors, and hinges. He may also help you locate your next layer of security: a safe.

SAFES

A good quality safe is a necessity in the pawnshop business. Once you've decided to become a pawnbroker, you should immediately start looking for a good safe. It is most economical to buy a used one. These are sometimes available in the classified section of your local newspaper if you live in a larger urban area, but if you live in a rural area, you might have a hard time finding a used one. I list sources for buying new safes in Appendix B. Some of these sources will even give credit terms.

I recommend buying the best safe you can afford. Your safe is the last layer of defense for your jewelry or anything else you can cram into it every night. I have read many stories about pawnbrokers in the Los Angeles area who were able to save their entire jewelry inventory during the 1992 riots because they had invested in good quality safes. Some of their stores had been burned to the ground, but their safes remained unopened and their contents untouched.

The safe I use is about 75 years old, and it weighs at least 2,500 pounds. I bought it through an ad in the local paper and paid $750 for it. At one time it was used by the treasurer of the city of Norfolk, Virginia. It

I bought this old safe for $750. It once belonged to the treasurer of the city of Norfolk, Virginia.

was the best safe I could afford when I first opened nine years ago, and though it has served me well, it's just about ready for retirement.

I also converted a large Snap-on toolbox for use as a gun safe. It has 11 drawers that are perfect for storing handguns and a large opening on top for other bulky items. It also holds all my gun cleaning gear and spare parts. I bought it from one of my customers for $250, and though it wasn't designed as a safe, it has a sturdy key lock and weighs more than 250 pounds empty. Once it is filled with handguns and locked, it is very difficult to carry off or get open.

This large Snap-on toolbox weighs more than 250 pounds empty and makes a great place to store handguns.

ALARM SYSTEMS

A good quality alarm system should be another layer of defense in your security plan. When I first opened my shop in 1984, I spent about $1,200 on a good electronic alarm system. Since then, I have spent another $1,500 on additional components and upgrades.

You should plan to spend at least $1,200 to $1,500 on your first system. It is best to contact several local alarm companies and get competitive bids. Make sure all bids include monitoring. I pay $21 per month to have my alarm system monitored. I also highly recommend having your system monitored by a company with a local monitoring switchboard.

The first company I used was sold to a national operation. I soon discovered that my alarm was being

A good alarm system is a necessity.

monitored from Atlanta, Georgia, and not locally as it had been. I got a call from the local sheriff's department one Christmas morning and was told that my alarm was going off and to call my alarm monitoring company. I then realized that the phone number I had been given by the sheriff's department was a toll-free number in Atlanta. (If you have ever tried to call anybody on Christmas day, you know how difficult it can be to get through.) After several attempts, I gave up and went to investigate myself. I discovered that it was the 7-11's alarm and not mine. If it had been my alarm, the alarm company would not have known and could not have called the police. Even if they did receive my signal, the delay would have added several minutes to the time it took for a lawman to arrive. Needless to say, I found a company with a local switchboard as soon as possible.

The manner in which you have your system monitored can also be important. I have two phone lines for my business, and I use one for my alarm system. This is the least expensive method, but it is vulnerable to thieves. If they cut my phone line between my shop and the pole, my alarm will automatically go off, but they can interrupt the system someplace else and bypass this function. You may opt for a cellular system, but I felt this was too costly for the minimal extra security it afforded.

Your system should also have a battery backup just in case there is power outage. My system will continue to operate for 12 hours after a power outage.

Never be cheap when it comes to buying an alarm system. I don't recommend buying one of those owner-installed systems from local hardware stores. Buy a good quality system from a reputable local company and have it installed and serviced by them.

My security system paid for itself one dark night about five years ago. Two criminals—one a local boy and the other a recently paroled felon from Maryland—decided to add my shop to their list of local business burglaries. They popped the lock on the front door of the business next door and ransacked it. Then they broke through the wall between our shops and triggered one of my motion sensors, which set off my alarm system. The alarm company's monitoring station called the sheriff's department and me. The deputy who responded to the alarm didn't notice anything awry and assumed it was a false alarm. I was informed that everything looked secure and that the alarm system had reset itself.

Twenty minutes later, the alarm went off again. This time when I was called, I went to investigate myself. When I arrived, I found that my shop had been burglarized. I concluded that the deputy had not gotten out of his car to investigate the first time. The burglars were probably still in the building when he came and waited until he left to continue. At that time, I kept my handguns in a showcase that I covered with a chain-link type cover. The burglars had enough time to pry this back and steal four handguns worth about $500. But the many layers of my defense system and the persistent shrill siren of my alarm kept these bums from taking much more. Two of the four handguns were eventually recovered.

Another problem that can occur with alarm systems is improperly placed sensors. My father built a specially designed building to house his pawnshop. It is made entirely out of 12-inch thick concrete block with reinforcement. The only glass in the entire building is two sets of double-glass doors with electric door openers. He hired a friend who is in the alarm business to install his new alarm system. (My father uses a dedicated phone line to monitor his system because he lives only a few blocks from his shop.) Two years later, a blind spot was discovered by a gang of thieves who chopped a hole through the roof of his building, lowered a person down a rope to the floor, and took several thousand dollars worth of handguns. (My father used to feel secure enough in his system to leave his handguns in their showcases at night.) If it were not for a passerby who happened to see the thieves in the store through the front doors, the theft would not have been discovered until the next day.

A good installer will not make these mistakes, but you should always check his work yourself. Passive infrared motion sensors should cover every square inch of your pawnshop. In addition, your system should have door/window contacts, horn/panel tamper switches, and a smoke detector. I have a horn siren inside my shop as well as outside to make any thieves that get in a little more uncomfortable. You can also have glass breakage sensors, wall shakers, and a panic button which will activate your alarm in case of an armed robbery.

PROTECTION AGAINST ARMED ROBBERIES

Armed robbery is another security concern, especially in rougher neighborhoods where most pawnshops are forced to locate because of zoning restrictions. I have situated my cash register and cash window at the rear of my showroom and placed a Lexan screen between me and the rest of the room. Lexan is bullet resistant and provides an effect that is rather bank-like without looking like a fortress. This gives me a secure area where I can handle cash and keep jewelry and other valuables out of reach. If you have to put your shop in a rough area, then you should probably consider designing a secure, bullet-resistant area to protect yourself.

While I was writing this book, one of the local pawnbrokers, who is located in the same part of town as my father, experienced an armed robbery. Just after the proprietor had opened his business for the day, three armed men came in and forced him and his clerk to the rear of the store and handcuffed them to a pole. The thieves took all his handguns, all his jewelry, and all the cash he had on hand. A fourth man waited in a car, and all four made a clean getaway. This pawnbroker was very lucky to have been spared his life, because many of these violent criminals will kill just so there are no witnesses. This pawnbroker did not carry a weapon, so he had no defense against these men.

My wife and I both carry sidearms at all times, and we both believe in the use of deadly force to protect our lives and the lives of our employees and customers. You should give serious consideration to becoming proficient in the use of firearms and discussing with employees a plan of action in case of an armed robbery. Just remember that complying with a robber's demands will not always insure your survival.

VIDEO SURVEILLANCE SYSTEMS

Video systems are another good idea if you can afford one. A professionally installed system is best, but an owner-installed system like mine can be adequate. I keep two cameras going around the clock, and though I can record off my system, I normally do not. One system was purchased at the local warehouse hardware store. The other is made up of a surveillance camera that I purchased through the pawnshop and an old black-and-white television. Thieves don't know if I'm recording them or not, so the deterrent effect is the same.

One camera covers the front door and a side room that I use for my music room. The monitor is next to the cash register facing away from the customers' line of sight, so they can tell they are being watched, but they can't see what's on the screen. The other monitor is in my office, so I can observe and listen to everything the camera covers without the subjects knowing they are being observed.

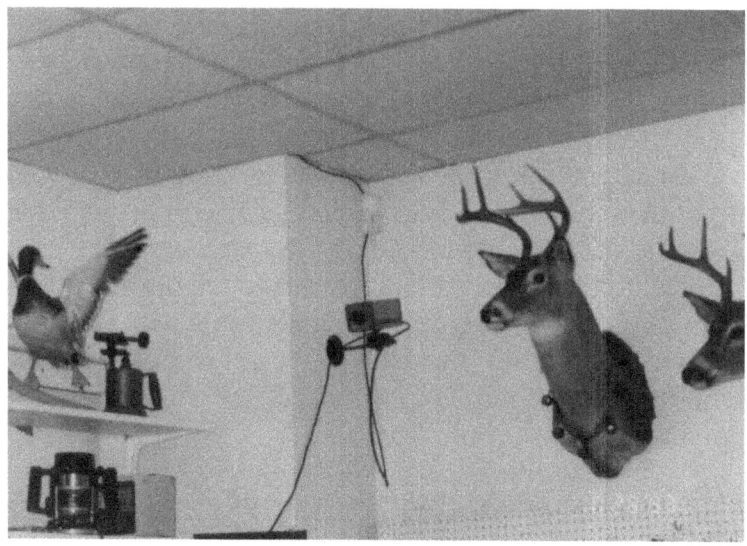

A video surveillance system can give you an extra set of eyes.

This entire system cost me about $400, and you can probably buy a new system with one monitor and two cameras for $500 to $600. I recommend using a videocassette recorder you've acquired through your shop to record with. Eight-hour Video Home System (VHS) tapes can be run during the workday, and by setting the timer on your VCR you can cover up to eight hours at night. Shoplifters are very wary of video cameras and normally will avoid stealing if they think they are being videotaped.

SECURITY TIPS

1) Never take cash home, and don't leave it in the store's safe. Make frequent bank deposits, but vary the times.

2) Be wary of people asking lots of questions, even if the queries seem friendly or innocent. A person who asks, "Do you have enough cash on hand to make a large loan?" or "Do you videotape all your transactions?" is a person to watch.

3) Drive different vehicles to work when possible. Watch for persons who may be following you home, and vary the routes you take home.

4) Avoid opening or closing alone. Follow team procedures similar to those used by banks. For example, when opening, one person checks the exterior, then the interior. After he is sure everything is okay, the second person is signaled to come in. The signal should be innocent in appearance and should be change periodically.

5) Keep an eye out for suspicious cars parked nearby or for a car that seems to be around frequently without good reason.

6) Let your family know when to expect you when you're coming or going. For instance, call home to let your spouse know when you leave and when you plan to arrive.

7) Don't encourage customers to contact you at home, and don't reveal personal information.

8) Create a code with your local constabulary for after-hours calls. This eliminates the possibility of a criminal impersonating a law officer calling you and asking you to come to the business, using an

apparent break-in or some other guise to lure you there.

9) Never leave a recording on your answering machine saying your business will be closed for a certain period of time.

10) Never leave a sign on your door saying you are closed because you are going out of town, on vacation, in the hospital, or anyplace a thief would think you won't be back from soon.

11) Protect exposed wiring for your alarm system on the exterior of your building. The wires can be cut easily and the sensors bypassed.

12) Don't be paranoid. BE AWARE AND BE PREPARED. Crime prevention and good security procedures can reduce a criminal's opportunities to rob, injure, or kill you, your family, or your employees.

4 How to Be a Pawnbroker

Loaning other people money is what pawnbroking is all about. You must loan out as much money as you can to be a successful pawnbroker. When these people come back, they repay these loans plus the interest due, or they pay the interest due to continue the loan. Interest can be your biggest source of profit because normally, 70 to 80 percent of all the loans you make will eventually be repaid. This means that only about one out of every four loans you make will be forfeited and provide merchandise for you to sell. Keep in mind that the more you loan or pay for something, the less you make when or if you have to sell it. You will still get a good supply of quality merchandise to sell, but most people won't give up their valuables for the amounts of money you will be lending them.

You should not enter into the business with the idea that you can legally steal everything that comes in your door to sell it and get rich quick. As a pawnbroker, you make contracts called pawn tickets with people that require you to return the property offered as collateral for a loan, which is called a pledge. Your

No

B
3571

DATE _10.5.93_ $ _2.00_

NAME _Demo_   ITEM _Dishwasher_

_____ Interest Paid For_____ Mos____

_____ Interest Paid For_____ Mos____

_____ Interest Paid For_____ Mos____

_____ Interest Paid For_____ Mos____

_____ Interest Paid For_____ Mos____

LICENSED AND BONDED BROKER
ALEXANDERS PAWN SHOP
Just off Interstate 64
Victor A. Cullen
867-8733   TABB Virginia 23602

1397 C Rt 17

Article _Yellow Sanyo Dishwasher_
and authorizes ALEXANDERS to deliver article to bearer of this ticket upon the
payment of

Amount Advanced $ _2.00_

Finance Charge Per Month $ _.40_

OTHER $ _2.00_

Total .... $

Joe Demo

_10-5_ 19 _92_

Ticket may be renewed upon the payment of interest. In the event of borrower failing
to repay or renew loan within _30 days_ or ALEXANDERS will declare
the pledge forfeited and put on public sale.

LIBERAL LOANS MADE ON GOODS OF ALL KINDS — ALSO BUY & SELL
WATCH YOUR TICKET DATE — WE DO NOT SEND NOTICES
NOT RESPONSIBLE FOR LOSS FROM
FIRE OR THEFT

No

B
3571

$3.00 SERVICE CHARGE FOR LOST TICKET
ALL BUSINESS STRICTLY PRIVATE.
NO GOODS SHIPPED C.O.D.
$2.00 UP EXTRA FOR PACKING.
INTEREST CAN BE PAID MONTHLY.

This is the old-style handwritten pawn ticket I used
several years ago.

A L E X A N D E R ' S   A M E R I C A N   P A W N   C O
Integrity
Loans • Buy • Sell
A Professional Broker
Licensed & Bonded

2715 George Washington Highway, Yorktown, VA 23693

STORE HOURS
Monday thru Friday 9:30 - 5:30
Saturday 10 - 2
Closed Sunday & Holidays

(804) 867-8733

ORIGINAL 30 DAY LOAN CONTRACT (YOU MUST HAVE FOR MERCHANDISE PICKUP)

I, JOE DEMO
CITY DUMP ACHILLES, VA.
hereby deposit with you the following described property:

residing at

Identification
VA 223232323

Account No: 000016024

DISCLOSURE STATEMENT
Amount financed 2.00
Interest 0.20
Ticket fee 2.00
Monthly service fee 0.20
Annual percent rate 120.00
TOTAL MONTHLY RENEWAL COST 2.40
===
PRINCIPAL, CHARGES & EXPENSES 4.40

DISHWASHER,SANYO, YELLOW

as security for the payment of a loan for the sum of   2.00 plus charges, payable on 00/00/00.
I warrant that I am the legal owner of said property and have the right to pledge same, and that there is no lein or mortgage
against same and I will defend my title and be responsible for the defense of same. I authorize ALEXANDER'S AMERICAN PAWN CO. to
deliver merchandise named on this ticket to bearer of same. We assume no liability if this ticket is lost or stolen. The amount you
received from this pawn transaction is considered to be the exact value of the pawned property.
Upon the Pledgor's failure to redeem or renew within the specified time, the pledge shall be forfeited to the Pawnbroker and all
right, title and interest to this property is thereafter divested.
All business strictly private. No pledges shown until redeemed. Watch your ticket date. We do NOT send notices.
The Pawnbroker is not responsible for loss due to fire or theft. I understand that there is a $2.00 charge for a lost ticket.
No items sent C.O.D. NO CHECKS!
The undersigned acknowledges receipt of the disclosures contained herein, and that this form was completed and all the blanks
were filled in prior to the undersigned executing same.

Signed _____

30 DAY LOAN
Acc.#: 000016024
10/05/92

This is the computer-printed pawn ticket I use now.

contract requires them to pay back the loan within an agreed upon time and/or pay the interest and other charges to continue the loan. If the person named on the pawn ticket fails to meet his obligations to you, then the property pledged may be put on public sale.

In my business, more than half of my income is from interest and other charges paid on loans. In fact, it is better for you if your borrowers repay their loans than not. It is true that you can normally make a good profit from the sale of unredeemed property, but once this property is gone, your customer can no longer use it to secure loans. This could actually be considered a loss.

For instance, Joe Emptypockets comes in for his usual once-a-month loan and pawns his class ring. If Joe gets a $20 loan and pays back $25 each month, that's a $60 per year profit. If you scrap Joe's ring as soon as you can, it would bring approximately $65 from a gold refinery at current market rates. Even though you would make an immediate profit of $45, you would make $15 less than what Joe would have paid in interest in a one-year period. Even if you let Joe pay a few days late, he'll still have his ring to pawn again.

I have many customers who pawn on a regular basis just like this, and as long as they don't take advantage of me, I let them have a little extra time. Each of us must determine what his limit is for this, but you will build a better customer base if you are a little lenient. As long as a customer calls or otherwise lets me know he will be late, I will give him extra time.

With my computer system, I am able to keep a record of transactions for each customer. This helps me decide when to pull a pledge. People who are regular customers and have a history of paying back

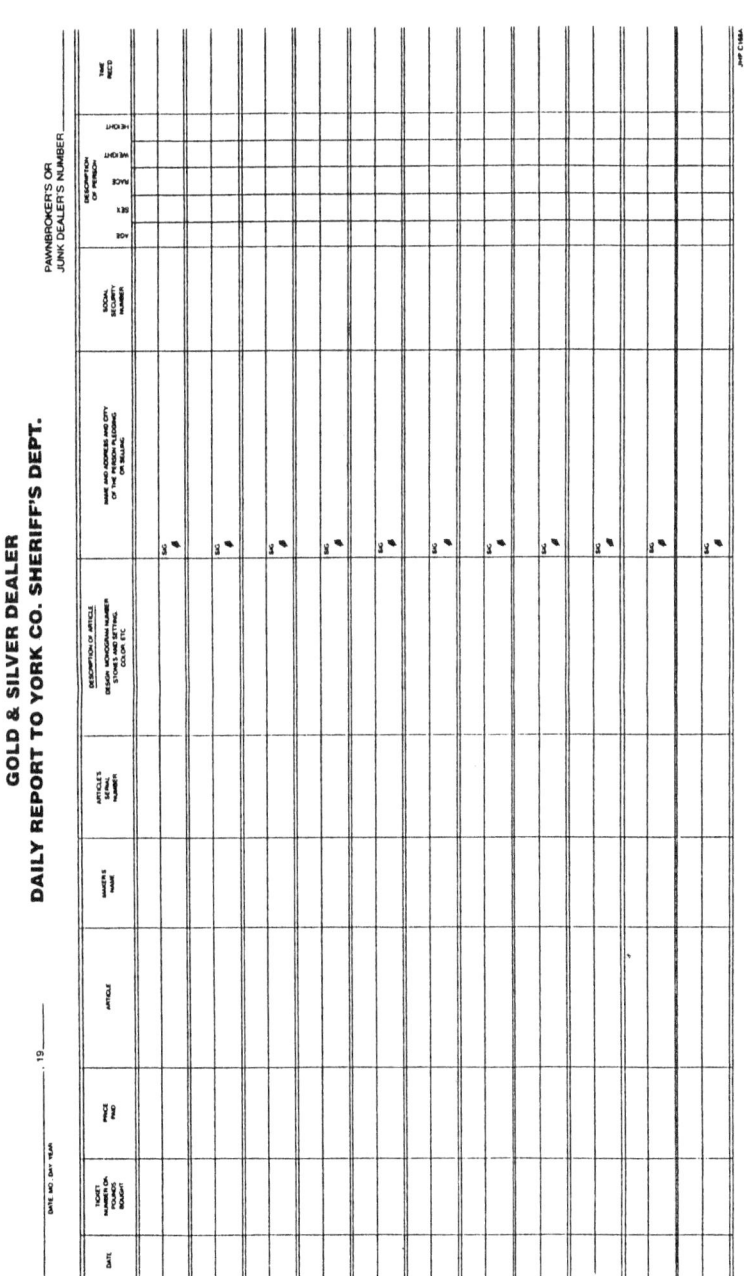

This is the sheet I used to keep records of all pawns made when I wrote my pawn tickets by hand.

My computer system with its pawnshop software are now the nerve center for my operation.

their loans will always be given special consideration. As for people who abuse my good nature and take advantage of me, selling their property is the fastest way to be rid of them. By conducting your business in this manner, you will grow an ever-expanding customer base. Return customers and their word-of-mouth advertising are business-building assets. You must treat people with kindness, compassion, and respect.

I get many new customers every day because some other pawnbroker was rude and nasty to them. When someone has to pawn their worldly possessions to make ends meet, they will naturally be anxious and embarrassed. You don't have to be their priest or psychiatrist, but listen to their stories politely, evaluate their merchandise, and give them a loan. If you do not want their merchandise, tell them why and decline the loan politely and diplomatically.

As for stories, I could write soap operas using all the hard luck, bad luck, and no luck stories I've heard. It is best to make your loans based strictly on the value of the merchandise in front of you. People will tell you anything to get your money. I always say that everyone's word is as good as his merchandise. That's why collateral used for a pawn is called a pledge. I must admit to an occasional charity loan, but there are plenty of government and private organizations that are available to help people. I prefer to donate money to these organizations and let them handle the charity cases. That way, I can be sure that the money is being used for a legitimate need and not for drugs or alcohol.

INTEREST

All of the interest rates and laws I quote in this book are current in the state of Virginia (see Appendix A). Every state in the union has its own laws governing pawnshops, but, for the most part, they are similar. As far as interest rates go, Virginia is probably on the low side. Virginia's interest rates are as follows.

Loan	Interest Rate
$0 to $25	10 percent per month
$25.01 to $99.99	7 percent per month
$100 or more	5 percent per month

Some states allow interest rates of 20 percent per month and higher, while some have rates even lower than Virginia's. We are allowed to charge a $2 ticket charge for the cost of writing a pawn ticket. We can also charge a reasonable rate for storage fees, appraisal fees, security fees, handling fees, maintenance fees, etc. Though state laws do mention storage fees, other charges are not mentioned. If you live in a state that allows 20 percent interest rates, then you do not need to be creative with other fees as we do. The present rates in Virginia were established back in the 1930s and are not sufficient to make a living. We must charge the customers for our services just like doctors and lawyers to achieve a rate of return on our money that is acceptable.

I appraise a piece of merchandise, write a legal contract to loan money on it, test it, pack it for long-term storage, store it, and maintain it in good condition. I also risk losing it if the police discover that it was stolen. I must pay for space, utilities, and 24-hour security. There are taxes, wages, and insurance to consider. All these services cost me money, and I must pass the cost on to my customers to make a profit. All these costs are shown on my pawn ticket as a monthly service fee. Combined with the legal Virginia interest rates and the $2 ticket fee, this amount is shown as a monthly renewal cost. The monthly renewal cost for Alexander's American Pawn Co. is as follows.

Loan	Interest	Service Fee	Ticket
$0 to $25	10 percent	10 percent	$2
$25.01 to $99.99	7 percent	9 percent	$2
$100 or more	5 percent	10 percent	$2

Every $25 loan I make gives me a legal profit of $84 per year. Every $50 loan I make gives me a profit of $120 per year. Every $100 loan I make gives me a $204

profit per year. The state sets four months as the normal loan term, unless the customer agrees to less time
which is not less than 30 days.

FEES

All my loans are written for 30 days, and the customer can pay a renewal fee to keep it longer. At the
rates I charge, you wouldn't think people would leave
anything in here very long, but I have loans that have
been here for more than six years. Just this morning,
a young man paid off his loan on a set of Bose speakers that had been here for three years. Even though he
made the loan at rates that were lower than what they
are now, he still paid a total of $682 in renewal fees
on a loan of $125. He was happy to get his speakers
back, and I expect to see him again for another loan. I
told him I would be glad to hold them for another
three years.

No investment I know of can pay you a better
return on your money than pawnbroking. Loans that
are paid on for long periods of time are the exception,
not the rule. Most people pay off their loans in less
than 30 days, and the rest within 90 days. When I first
opened, I gave people 90 days before they had to start
paying renewal fees. My father was giving 120 days.
We found this to be a burden on our customers
because they had to come up with more money, and it
was a burden on us because if the pledge was forfeited, we had an extra two or three months interest
invested in the property. We now write only 30-day
loans. If your state allows it, I recommend giving 30-
day loans. When you first open your pawnshop, you
will need a return on your money as soon as possible.

In addition to renewal fees, I also charge late fees if a person does not return the loan in the original 30 days or does not pay a renewal fee on time. I usually allow an extra five to seven days, but you have to think about getting interest on the interest if they are any later than that. I normally charge a $5 late fee on loans of more than $50, but I rarely charge these late fees for loans under this amount. If these late-paying people are willing pay fees covering two months, I will normally drop the late fee. Although most are glad to pay late fees to save their property, it is good business to give as many breaks as you can stand. I think of it as paying for the good "word-of-mouth" advertising.

The only other fees I am able to charge are lost ticket fees and shipping fees if the loan is paid off by mail and I must ship the customer's property to him. I don't usually charge the lost ticket fees unless I'm angered.

HOW MUCH TO LOAN?

Assessing how much money to loan on something is a very important skill to master as a pawnbroker. Generally, I try to loan the least amount that people will accept. The less you loan on something, the less interest you will make, but, on the other hand, you will make more profit if you have to sell the item. You must also consider how much you can afford to lose if the property turns out to be stolen and is confiscated by police. You should, of course, base most of this on the cost of the merchandise, but which cost?

There is a suggested retail price from the manufacturer, and there is a discount or wholesale price that most things sell for. As a dealer, you can buy most things at wholesale price. I base the amount I loan on an item on how much I believe I can sell that item for in my store. I will loan 30 to 50 percent of that price. This enables me to get a 50 to 70 percent profit margin (a 100 to 200 percent markup), which is necessary to be successful. (I explain how to value specific items in later chapters.) The following is what a typical transaction looks like in my business.

At about 10:00 A.M. a man and his young child come into my shop. I ask him if I can help him, and he says he needs a loan. The man has a Pioneer compact disk (CD) player and a small cardboard box with assorted jewelry in it. While I look over his merchandise, he tells me that he missed a week of work and needs some extra money to pay his light bill. The man's property looks promising, so I ask him the big question: "How much do you need?" This is always the first question I ask a potential customer unless he has taken out a loan before. If so, I will ask the borrower if he wants the same amount as the last loan. New customers will sometimes reply with a reasonable amount, but normally they say, "As much as possible," or they will ask, "How much can you give me?" This man tells me he needs $170. I prefer people to tell me how much they need up front so we don't waste time. If it's a reasonable amount, I will give it to them. If not, and they won't consider less money, then there is no need to go any further. It is best to not consider the reason people tell you they need the money, and, instead, base what you pay strictly on the value of the property they offer.

I always remind people that the less money they borrow, the easier it is to get their property back. I sometimes hurt people's feelings when I make them offers on their merchandise, and they leave in a huff, only to return later to accept my offers. You will lose some borrowers this way, but you have to do things that are to your benefit, not theirs.

The man who needs $170 pulls some jewelry out of his cardboard box for me to appraise for a loan. I weigh his jewelry, examine the stones, and offer him $120 because I estimate that it could sell for at least $240 as scrap or as much as $360 in my jewelry showcase. I hook up his CD player and run a disk on it. After I determine that it works properly, I offer him an additional $30 loan because I estimate that I could sell the CD player for $60 to $80. Even though this only totals $150, he accepts the loan.

This scenario will probably be the norm for most of your new customers. Some people even ask for more than they actually need and expect to be talked down. When it comes to repeat customers (who are the majority of my customers), I will normally repeat their previous loan. Since I have computerized my shop, I can look up previous transactions and write new loans with a few key strokes.

5 Jewelry

Gold. The word conjures up visions of prospectors digging large nuggets of yellow metal out of sluice pans or of a pirate's treasure glistening on a coral reef below azure waters. The discovery of gold in your pawnshop won't be quite as romantic, but you will not have to risk your life or even get dirty to profit from it. People will bring you all types of gold objects, and most of them will have some type of precious or semiprecious jewel in them. For your benefit, you should consider diamonds to be precious stones; rubies, sapphires, and emeralds to be semiprecious; and everything else to be not worth much.

Learn all you can about diamonds, gems, and gold. It is helpful to go to other pawnshops and jewelry stores to see what they charge for their jewelry. Go to large jewelers and ask to look at their diamonds. It is also good to keep on hand several discount department store catalogs that have color pictures of their jewelry. I find that I can buy most jewelry for about 10 cents on the dollar of what it sold for new. I can usually sell it for 50 percent or less than what the jewelry stores ask. Even the discount chains like Wal-Mart and Kmart can't compete with that.

Below are the basic tools you will need to weigh, measure, and otherwise work with gold jewelry, diamonds, and other gems.

> scales
> electronic gold tester
> electronic diamond tester
> 10X loupe
> accurate diamond gauge
> Moe diamond gauge and calculator
> ultrasonic jewelry cleaner
> buffing machine and accessories
> ring clamp
> needle-nose pliers
> jeweler's saw and blades

Equipment for weighing gold.

At the top of the list are scales. You will need scales that meet legal-for-trade specifications for your state. They should weigh grams, troy ounces, and pennyweight. They need not be the most expensive, but they should be sturdy and durable. You will likely be using them every day. When shopping for this equipment, I usually buy models that fall in the middle of the price range. I provide several sources for jeweler's supplies in Appendix C.

I still have the Ohaus triple beam scales that I started out with more than nine years ago. They still work perfectly but are slow and tedious to use. I've been spoiled since I acquired my digital scales. It's nice to have an instant reading of weight without changing little weights and sliding little scales and reading hash marks to get an exact measurement. That's why I suggested that you buy a modern scale with a digital readout.

As far as which weight system to use, I recommend that you use troy. I was trained in the troy system, and I don't care much for gram measurements. Gold is always traded in the world markets in troy ounces. Sometimes you may have to convert to gram weight for your customers, but digital scales can do this, which is another good reason to own one. Some pawnbrokers buy and sell by gram weight, and customers may be price shopping. Also, many of the discount jewelers sell their gold by the gram. Here are some basics:

> one troy pound = 12 troy ounces
> one troy ounce = 20 pennyweight (dwt)
> one pennyweight = 24 grains
> 15.43 grains = one gram (gm)
> one gram = 1.6 pennyweight (approx.)
> 31.1 grams = one troy ounce

GOLD

If you want to be a successful pawnbroker, you will need to follow the price of gold carefully. The London market sets the daily price per troy ounce for gold in the world markets. This is referred to as the London "fix" and it is done twice a day. This price is for the spot market, which means this is the price you will pay if you take possession of the gold that day. This daily price quote is reported on radio and television financial programs and is published in the newspaper under metal commodities. These quotes will determine what you should pay and, to some extent, what you can sell your scrap gold and retail jewelry for. Though gold is traded in the market in troy ounces, the main unit of measurement you need to be concerned about is the pennyweight. Almost all the buying and selling of gold in your pawnshop will be done by pennyweight.

How Much to Pay for Gold

How much you pay for gold in your pawnshop should be determined more by what you can scrap it for and less by what you think you may be able to retail it for as jewelry. It's true I will pay more for a nice resalable piece of jewelry than a piece that is good only for scrap, but I always pay less than gold value at the current market rate. To figure out the gold value for a specific piece of jewelry, you must begin by looking at the current market price. For example, if the current market price is $368 per troy ounce, you must divide by 20 to get the price per pennyweight (dwt), which is $18.40. You should consider the profit margin of the refiner to which you will sell it. (Some refiners are listed in

Appendix C.) Most refiners will pay at least 95 percent of spot price for a 5 percent profit margin. (The amount will vary according to the amount you scrap, and there are sometimes other fees involved.) So $18.40 per pennyweight multiplied by 95 percent is $17.48. This is what you can realistically expect to sell gold for in the spot market on this particular day. You must also figure that on the day you actually sell your gold, the price may have changed. What will the price be tomorrow? If I were able to predict the answer to that question, I could be as rich as Ross Perot.

The price of gold fluctuates due to the influence of many different forces. Sometimes emotion or panic in world markets, political upheavals, and wars can affect prices. A strike in a gold-producing state like South Africa or a shooting war in an oil-producing state like Kuwait will cause gold prices to go up. A big sell-off of gold by Russia or a large bank will cause gold prices to go down. Gold has always been used as a hedge against inflation, and this can also have a big effect on prices. You have no control over these things, so you must watch trends in the market and situations in the world to determine what percentage of spot market price you are willing to pay.

When you are in the gold business, it pays to watch the news. You must also consider that, at least in most cases, the gold you get from your customers is not pure gold; it is mixed with alloys. You will occasionally see gold bullion or gold coins, but mostly you get karat gold in the form of jewelry. European-made jewelry will be marked with the percentage of pure gold contained in the piece instead of a karat mark (k) like American jewelry. Here is a listing of karat marks and corresponding European marks and percentages of pure gold:

U.S.A.	European	Percentage
24k	999	99.9
18k	750	75
14k	585	58.5
10k	417	41.7
8k	333	33.3

Since the Persian Gulf war, I have seen a lot of 22k gold jewelry that was brought back by servicemen from Saudi Arabia. These pieces are sometimes marked as 90 percent, or 900. There is also dental gold (yes, people really do take the gold out of dead people's teeth), which is usually 16k or 65 percent gold.

Once you figure out what karat gold you are working with, you have to decide how much per pennyweight you want to pay for it. For example, a customer brings you a 10k yellow gold class ring with a red stone in it, and it weighs in at 10 dwt. The red stones in 99 percent of all class rings are synthetic rubies and are worth practically nothing for scrap. You must estimate the weight of the stone and deduct that amount from the total weight of the ring. If the stone weighs 1.5 dwt, then the gold in the ring weighs 8.5 dwt. Next, you will need to figure the price per dwt for 10k gold, which is 41.7 percent pure gold. $17.48 per dwt (the previously determined gold value for that day) times 41.7 percent equals $7.29 per dwt. This is the price per pennyweight you will receive from the refiner on the day he receives it from you if the spot price is $368 per ounce. I will normally pay $3.50 to $4.50 per pennyweight for a ring like this. This works out to $30 for a loan, or $35 to $40 to buy it. This leaves me room to still make a profit even if gold goes down in value.

I always try to buy and pawn jewelry at prices that enable me to make a profit at scrap. If I am able to sell a piece at retail, then it's a big bonus. Retail jewelry can bring double or triple its scrap value. If you do decide to send gold to a refiner for scrap, you should wait until you have at least 100 dwt. My refiner pays up to 95 percent of spot price on shipments over 100 dwt.

At the prices discussed earlier, I would receive about $62 ($7.29 x 8.5 = $61.97) for the class ring. I could make as much as a $32 profit on this ring if he doesn't redeem it, or if he leaves it in pawn and pays interest, I could make $6.80 per month. In just five months, I can make even more than if I had scrapped it. Here are some formulas to use when trading in gold:

spot price of gold ÷ 20 dwt = spot price per dwt
spot price per dwt x karat percentage = karat price per dwt
karat price per dwt x 95 percent = price per dwt from refiner

I don't usually go through all these calculations. Instead, I rely on the following table unless I have a difficult customer who has had offers from other dealers and I must offer a better price.

10k	$3 to $3.50 per dwt
14k	$5 to $5.50 per dwt
18k	$6.50 to $7 per dwt
22k	$8 to $8.50 per dwt
24k	$9 to $10 per dwt

I have been pawning and buying gold for more than nine years, and spot prices have varied from just under $300 per ounce to just over $400 per ounce. I have always paid about the same prices that are listed above, and I have always made a profit.

Testing for Fakes

Another thing to beware of when buying gold is fakes. It may look like gold, feel like gold, and even be marked with a karat mark, but it still may turn out not to be gold. Even after years of experience, I have been fooled.

With the new electronic gold testers that are now on the market, testing gold is fast, easy, and accurate. The tester I have works by placing the piece to be tested on a tray and attaching an alligator clip, which is wired to the positive lead, to the piece. The negative lead is wired through a tube that contains a special gel. Twisting the back of this tube dispenses a drop of this gel, and the authenticity and karat value of the piece is tested by

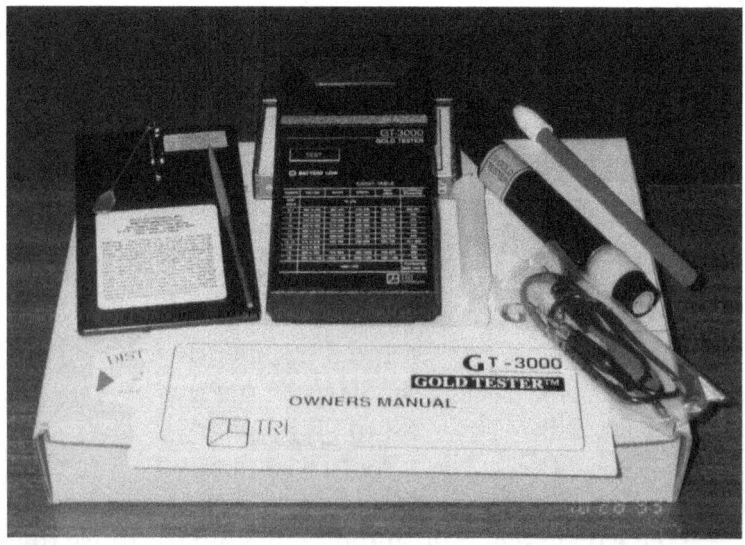

Gold testers.

touching the drop of gel away from the point where the piece contacts the alligator clamp. You then press the test button to get a numerical reading, which is compared to a scale that gives you a karat value. This is a vast improvement over the old method of acid testing.

To acid test a piece of gold, you must have a file and some nitric acid. You must file into the piece to get through any layers of gold plating and then apply the acid to the bare metal. Gold will keep the acid clear, silver will turn it yellow, and other metals will turn it green. To determine the karat value, the piece must be rubbed on a touchstone, acid applied, and the colors interpreted. These methods are time consuming and inaccurate. Even if you can file an area that won't be noticed, you will still leave an ugly mark on the jewelry. Some customers won't allow you to do this to their jewelry, which leaves you with the choice to either not take it or not test it.

For years, I got by without using an electronic tester, but if I had tested a few of the fakes I took, the tester would have easily paid for itself. Most of the time, I can tell that a piece is real, but if there is any question in my mind at all, I run it on my tester. I highly recommend that you buy an electronic gold tester and use it often until you gain enough experience to do without it. It is also a good idea to weigh the jewelry and reach an agreement with the customer for a price before you do your testing. After you've had enough experience, you will be able to tell the good from the bad about 99 percent of the time. Most gold-plated jewelry will be marked as such. Some of these markings are:

> 1/10 12k (14k, 18k, 24k) G.F.
> 1/20 12k (14k, 18k, 24k) G.F.

G.F.
Gold Filled
R.G.P.
Rolled Gold Plated
Heavy Gold Electroplate
10k, 14k, 18k, or 24k H.G.E.

When you see a piece marked 14kp or 18kp, it does-n't mean that it is plated, but that it is "plumb" gold. Plumb means that the gold content is exactly the karat marked. In 1976, Congress amended the National Gold and Silver Act, and by 1981, all American gold manufac-turers had to adhere to the stricter standards for gold content in their jewelry. Previously, for example, jewelry manufacturers could mark their jewelry as 14k when it was actually only 13k. Since 1981, all American jewelry manufacturers have marked their jewelry with the plumb designation.

Sometimes you will encounter silver jewelry that is gold plated. This is also called gold overlay. This type of jewelry isn't usually marked as plated but is marked with the designation 925. This means the piece is 92.5 percent silver. Look for plated jewelry to show peeling and wear if it's been worn often. These things will show even better if you look at it closely with your loupe.

In my experience, gold chains are the items most often faked. Most gold chains are soldered on their ends, or, at the very least, the ring that attaches the clasp to the chain is soldered. While this isn't always proof positive that you have the genuine article, it is a good indicator. I have taken fake chains that look real even to the soldered ends. The last ones I took seemed to tarnish after I kept them the required 30 days.

When I took them in, I failed to test them with my acid (I didn't have an electronic tester at the time). They were marked 14k, and they had nice lobster-claw clasps on them, but they were not gold. They were evidently gold-plated brass that were made specifically to rip off people like me who buy gold. This $275 lesson was enough to convince me to buy an electronic gold tester. From then on, any piece of jewelry, especially chains, that weighs more than 5 dwt or that wasn't previously pawned by a regular customer gets checked on my electronic gold tester.

Other frequently faked items are gold watches. There are a few problems that can be encountered. Gold watches are hard to authenticate even with a gold tester. The tester may damage the delicate moving parts or the crystal of the watch. Only the case of the watch is actually gold and can't be weighed accurately unless you take the moving parts out, which is impractical. If the customer gives you permission to file a small notch where the band is attached underneath the watch, you can put a tiny amount of acid in the notch to check for a reaction. You must take the band off to do this, and you must be careful not to damage the watch. If the band is soldered to the watch and is marked as gold, you can usually put the band in your electronic tester and get an accurate reading. Again, get permission from the customer, and let him or her know that you can't be responsible for damage, though you will do your best not to do any.

If a customer won't let you test his watch in these ways, you may want to pass on it unless you can get it cheap. It is always best to stay low in your pricing on gold watches so you can't get burned by a fake. Any watch that has a stainless steel back, except a Rolex, is not gold. If you can test the diamonds and they are good, then this is usually a sign that the watch is gold, if it is marked as such. You will see many more ladies' watches than men's watches, and luckily they aren't faked as often. The best advice I can give on watches is to be careful. There are huge profits to be made on watches, but if you get a fake, there are also huge losses to be suffered.

If you are not well acquainted with jewelry, it is in your best interest to check most everything that comes into your shop until you are confident that you can spot fakes. Even then, you will want to check anything that looks suspicious in any way. It only takes a loss on one fake to cancel out the profit on several good deals.

Scrapping Gold for Cash

Selling your gold to a refiner is a good, dependable source of quick cash when you need it. Though I try to sell my scrap gold when the market price is high, I am not always able to hold out for the best price. Most of the time, I end up selling right before my quarterly estimated income tax is due, but sometimes I hold out to hit a peak in market prices. I recently sent off a batch of scrap to my refiner and got a check back for more than $6,000. I hit a market price of around $380 per ounce. I had been holding out for a higher price, but when it peaked at just over $400 per ounce then fell back down, I jumped in and sold. If I had sold when the market was $20 per ounce higher, I could have made an extra $200. All the same, I made at least a $2,700 profit on this sale.

You should try to save every piece of jewelry you can to fill your jewelry showcases with merchandise for retail. I scrap only what I can't use in this capacity,

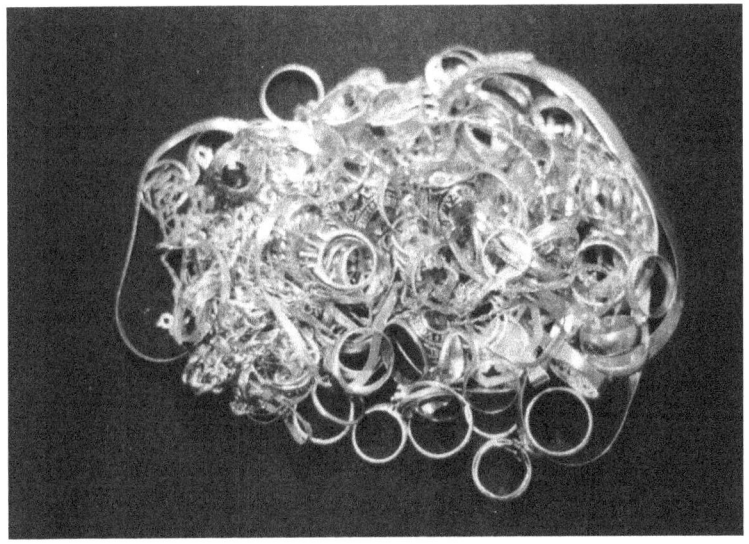

Gold! These pieces are headed for the refinery.

which includes broken and kinked chains, class rings, wedding bands, rings that are worn or broken, and any other jewelry that isn't suitable for sale. I will also, on occasion, take a diamond out of its mounting to scrap (this is covered later) and use the mounting for gold scrap. Some pawnbrokers try to sell wedding bands for retail, but I find them hard to sell and mostly use them for scrap.

DIAMONDS

Diamonds conjure up visions of wealth and beauty. They inspire awe and mystery in people. Most people consider them to be the most valuable objects in the world, but diamonds are nothing but rocks, mere pieces of stone. When cut and polished correctly, they are things of beauty, but there is nothing mysterious or magical about them. The fact that they are valuable and expensive is a testament to the public relations campaign put on by the De Beers diamond cartel. I won't get into the saga of the De Beers family or a history of the diamond industry, but it is sufficient to say they are responsible for making the diamond what it is today.

The De Beers control 90 percent of all the world's diamonds, either in their own vaults or in the countries where the world's diamonds are produced. By controlling supply and, through continuous commercial campaigns, demand, this diamond cartel has kept the price of diamonds artificially high. Everyone knows diamonds are forever, diamonds are a girl's best friend, and that if a man loves a woman he must give her a diamond. The De Beers have convinced us that diamonds are extremely rare, when in reality they are only rare because the diamond cartel strictly controls supply. If the diamond cartel ever ceases to exist, the price of diamonds would probably fall close to the price of rubies, sapphires, and emeralds.

Watch the news and trade magazines for anything about Russian diamonds. I have heard rumors about them dumping diamonds on the world market. The Russians have more diamonds stockpiled than any other country or organization (including De Beers), and they are in terrible financial shape. If they begin dumping, the price of diamonds could plummet. This could have a bad effect on your business, cause people to lose confidence in diamonds, and wreck the whole diamond industry.

In the meantime, you can make large amounts of money buying and selling diamonds. Since the De

Beers cartel controls the supply of diamonds, they also control the price. There is no spot market or London fix for diamonds like there is for gold. You can't check the TV or the local newspaper for a daily quote on the price of diamonds.

The price of diamonds is affected by the famous four "Cs." These are carat, color, clarity, and cut. Of course, the price of a raw uncut diamond is only affected by the last three Cs, but you will likely never see a raw diamond, so I will explain the basics about finished diamonds. The basics should be enough to get you started, but I recommend that you read the books listed in Appendix C for more detailed information, because it would take volumes to teach everything about this subject.

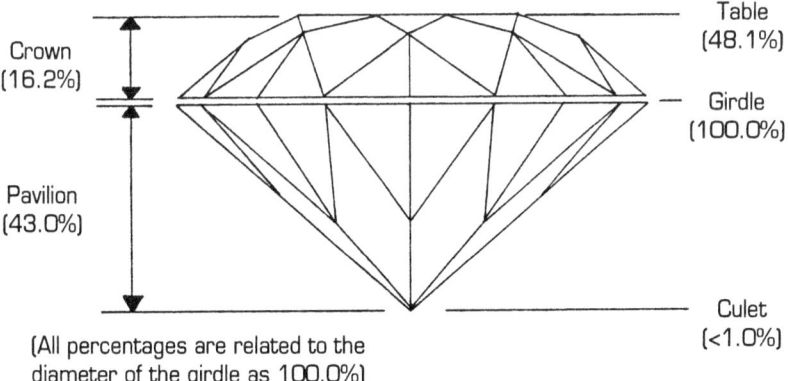

Crown (16.2%)

Pavilion (43.0%)

Table (48.1%)

Girdle (100.0%)

Culet (<1.0%)

(All percentages are related to the diameter of the girdle as 100.0%)

Parts of a finished diamond. This is how a perfect round-cut diamond should look.

Carat

Let me first deal with what a carat is. Notice that it is spelled with a "c" and not a "k." Diamonds are weighed in carats, and the content of gold in a piece of jewelry is measured in karats. It is not necessary to buy a scale to weigh diamonds, because most times you will be dealing with mounted stones, and you can only estimate the weight if the stone is attached to a ring. It would be convenient to have a carat scale to weigh loose stones, but I have always gotten by without one. A carat is broken down into points so that 1 ct equals 100 pts. The corresponding fractional carats are also broken down into points. These are:

$$
\begin{array}{rcl}
7/8 \text{ ct} & = & 85 \text{ to } 90 \text{ pts} \\
3/4 \text{ ct} & = & 75 \text{ pts} \\
3/5 \text{ ct} & = & 60 \text{ pts} \\
1/2 \text{ ct} & = & 50 \text{ pts} \\
3/8 \text{ ct} & = & 40 \text{ pts} \\
1/3 \text{ ct} & = & 33 \text{ pts} \\
1/4 \text{ ct} & = & 25 \text{ pts} \\
1/5 \text{ ct} & = & 20 \text{ pts} \\
1/8 \text{ ct} & = & 12 \text{ pts} \\
1/10 \text{ ct} & = & 10 \text{ pts}
\end{array}
$$

Color

The next thing to consider is color. Diamonds come in several colors besides white. I have seen diamonds as blue as sapphires, as brown as rusty water, as green as emeralds, and as yellow as sunflowers. These are usually called fancy-color diamonds, and they can be worth more than their counterpart, which is white. Most of the stones I see that have color are not fancy colored but just off color. This is not a good thing. I always pay less for off-color diamonds. The closer a diamond is to being colorless the better. I'm sure you've heard of diamonds being blue/white. This doesn't mean the diamond has a blue tint but that it is nearly colorless. Color can have a big effect on the value of a diamond, maybe even more than the other Cs. The Gemological Institute of America (GIA), an appraiser's association, rates the color of diamonds on a scale from D through Z+.

D E F	G H I J K L M	N O P	Q R S T U V	W X Y Z Z+
color-less	near colorless	faint yellow	very light yellow	light yellow

Clarity

The third factor to consider when buying diamonds is clarity. When diamonds were formed millions of years ago, most of them trapped small particles of carbon inside. These flaws look like tiny pieces of coal, air spaces, fractures, or small feathers.

If no flaws can be seen with a 10X loupe, then the diamond is said to be flawless. There is really no such thing as a flawless diamond, because if you have a strong enough microscope, flaws can be seen in every diamond. The following is the GIA scale for clarity and the corresponding descriptions:

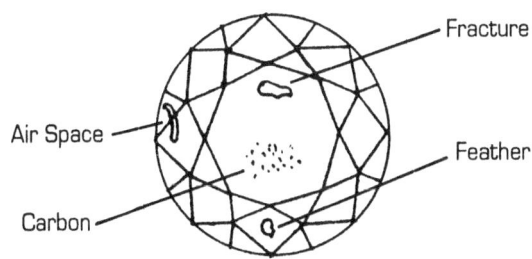

Common diamond flaws.

Clarity Grade	Description
F (Flawless)	No visible inclusions at 10X. Okay on tiny natural (part of the original surface of the diamond that is not removed when the stone is polished), but nothing visible internally or externally.
IF (Internally Flawless)	Very minor surface blemish removable with recut or polishing. Value usually at weight of recut gem.
VVS 1 (Very, Very Slightly Included)	No table involvement. Very tiny pit, scratch, embedded crystal (must be under crown facets).
VVS 2 (Very, Very Slightly Included)	One tiny inclusion: pit, spot, cleave, feather, abrasion, small extra facet.
VS 1 (Very Slightly Included)	Combination totaling two tiny spots in table: crystal, bearding (tiny fractures on the girdle), fracture, cleavage, bigger natural, scratch group.
VS 2 (Very Slightly Included)	Combination totaling three table inclusions, if not in the center: cluster, bigger crystal, feather, bearding more prominent. Large extra facets.
SI 1 (Slightly Included)	Combination totaling four of the following: series of nicks, scratch

group, inclusion cluster, small spot group in center of table.

SI 2 (Slightly Included)	Combination totaling five of the following: inclusions in table center, major flaws, cloudy area, inclusion cluster, large embedded crystals, carbon spots, cleavage visible.
I 1 (Included)	Combination totaling six of the following: dead spots in stone (areas that block reflected light: cleavages, feathers, embedded crystals, carbon spots, cloudy sections
I 2 & I 3 (Included)	Lowest GIA clarity grades. Any combination of inclusions totaling seven or more.

Cut

The final C is cut. The way a diamond is cut can mean the difference between a brilliant sparkle of reflected light and a dull fish-eye appearance. The cut of a diamond probably has the least effect on its price but is still an important factor. Modern faceting machines are now used to cut diamonds, but fallible men run them. There are precise specifications for every style of diamond cut, but these measurements are often impossible for the diamond cutter to achieve. The diamond cutter tries to end up with the largest stone he can get from a raw diamond, but he must also try to cut off any flaws he can. Sometimes the result is less than perfect and can affect the value of the stone.

Evaluating Diamonds

There is a standard procedure I use to evaluate a diamond ring to be pawned or sold. I check the karat marking and weigh the piece to determine its gold value. If the mark is difficult to read, I use my 10X loupe.

With my loupe still at hand, I use it and my diamond gauge to estimate the approximate weight of the stone. By holding the gauge over the diamond, looking at it through my loupe, and moving the gauge until I find the hole that the diamond completely fills, I can make a fairly accurate guess on the weight of the stone. The stone must completely fill the hole, leaving no space around the edge. The gauge gives readings in points. Occasionally, I get a ring that is marked inside with its weight in points. When I find this, it gives me a good idea of how accurately I'm estimating the weight of diamonds using my gauge. When a ring has more than one diamond, I estimate the weight of each one, then add these together for a total weight. Sometimes it's hard to get the gauge right on top of small diamonds, so I get as close as possible or sometimes next to the stone and compare the stone to the holes and take a guess. I find that in most cases, diamonds in clusters have even sizes like 1/4 ct, 1/2 ct, 1 ct, etc.

When I look at a stone with my loupe, I also check for flaws and damage. Always check very carefully for damage, especially around the girdle of the stone. The girdle is the part of a diamond that is easiest to damage. This area is very thin, and people chip their diamonds through abuse or neglect and never even realize they've done it. I have also seen chips in diamonds that occurred either before or during mounting and were hidden under a prong. A diamond that is chipped is worth considerably less than one of equal quality that is not chipped. A severely chipped diamond can be almost worthless.

Severely included diamonds are also something to watch out for. In the past couple of years, I've seen more of what I call "promotional diamonds." These are really trashy stones of such poor quality that they look like cut and polished gravel. They are usually cut in countries where labor is extremely cheap, like India, Pakistan, or Thailand. I will take these pieces in pawn, but I base the amount given for them mainly on the gold weight. I rarely find diamonds that don't have some kind of flaw, and I can't ever recall getting any diamonds that meet the GIA criteria for a flawless rating. I usually figure that minor flaws in stones smaller than 20 pts have little effect on value. When the stone is larger than 20 pts, flaws start to make a big difference.

I also make a judgment about the cut and color of a diamond while estimating its weight and looking for flaws. These are difficult qualities to appraise unless you've been to GIA school. To check the color of a diamond, place a piece of white paper behind it, and look at it under good natural light.

How Much to Pay for Diamonds

The value of a diamond increases geometrically according to its size, not arithmetically. For example, a 1-ct diamond could be worth four times as much as a 1/2-ct diamond of equal quality instead of twice as much, even though it is only twice as large. I use a pricing scale similar to the one shown below:

Weight	Price
1 pt to 20 pts	25 cents to $1 per pt
20 pts to 25 pts	50 cents to $2 per pt
25 pts to 50 pts	$1 to $4 per pt
50 pts to 75 pts	$2 to $5 per pt
75 pts to 100 pts	$3 to $7 per pt
100 pts and larger	$4 to $10 per pt (more for a stone larger than 2 ct)

These prices are, of course, for individual stones and not for the total weight of a cluster. For example, a customer comes into my store with a ladies' 25-pt solitaire engagement ring that weighs 1 pennyweight. The stone has a few specks of carbon but is cut well and appears to be near colorless. I offer the customer $40 for a loan and $50 to buy it. (Before handing over the cash, check the stone on the diamond tester by touching the diamond with the probe on the tester while holding the ring.) If the ring became available for sale, I would put it in my showcase and ask $200 for it, or I could scrap it for $70 to $100. If the ring had a cluster of five stones that had the same total weight, I would offer $20 for a loan and $25 to buy it. It would retail in my showcase for $60 to $75 and scrap for $30 or $40.

When it comes to larger diamonds like 1/3 ct, 1/2 ct, 3/4 ct, 1 ct, and larger, your knowledge of diamonds becomes more important. I can buy a 1/3-ct stone for $60, a 1/2-ct stone for $150 to $200, a 3/4-ct stone for $250 to $350, and a 1-ct stone for $500 to $700. The largest stone I ever bought was a 1 1/2-ct heart-shaped diamond. It was cut well and was really white, and I paid $1,500 for it. Of course, my wife liked it, so I gave it to her.

Scrapping Diamonds

Diamonds can be scrapped just like gold, though the selection of buyers is more limited. When scrapping diamonds, you must be extremely careful not to chip or otherwise damage them when removing them from their mountings. You will need a ring clamp, needle-nose pliers, and a jeweler's saw.

Rings with Tiffany-style four- or six-prong mountings are easy to remove. Tightly clamp the ring in the ring clamp and, using the pliers, carefully pry the prongs away from the diamond. Gold is a soft metal and bends fairly easily, so you don't have to be Arnold Schwarzenegger to bend it. When the diamond becomes loose, dump it into a small Ziplock bag. Be careful not to drop it on the floor, because once on the ground, diamonds are very hard to find. I have dropped several small diamonds around my jewelry bench and never found them.

Diamonds mounted in other ways usually have to be cut out with a jeweler's saw. If you are going to scrap a ring, don't worry about tearing it up to get the diamond out. Just be concerned about damaging the diamond. The saw blade won't cut the diamond, although the diamond will dull the blade in a hurry. Try to cut only the metal holding the diamond in the mount. I sometimes find it helpful to use an engraving tool with a flat point to finish cutting the stones loose. If you have a large stone you want to scrap but are afraid to cut it out of the mounting, most of the buyers I list in Appendix C will take it out for you and pay you for the scrap. The only disadvantage is that you won't get top dollar for your scrap gold. A short course in jewelry repair would teach this process.

One more thing—be sure to use your diamond

tester before buying any diamonds. It is really embar-
rassing to send a diamond off for scrap only to be
informed that it is a fake.

RUBIES, SAPPHIRES, AND EMERALDS

When buying or pawning gold jewelry with rubies,
sapphires, or emeralds in them, I don't add much
over the price of the gold in which they are mounted.
The reason is that I have not found a buyer for these
stones as scrap, and I value jewelry more for its scrap
value than its artistic value. Don't get me wrong,
these are rare and desirable gems, and they are sal-
able as jewelry, but they must be acquired cheaply to
be profitable. There are also a lot of fakes out there. A
diamond can be tested on a diamond tester, and gold
can be tested on a gold tester, but colored gems are
hard to authenticate. You almost have to be a gemol-
ogist to distinguish the real from the fake colored
gemstones.

Evaluating Colored Gems
I use my diamond gauge to size colored gems, but
the holes in it do not give an accurate estimate of their
weight, because they are calibrated for diamonds.
Colored gems are weighed in carats, but a carat of diamonds is different from a carat of colored gems. Like a
diamond, the weight of a colored gem has an effect on
its value, and its value tends to grow geometrically with
its size. In my opinion, though, size doesn't make a difference until a gem weighs more than half a carat. I also
think emeralds are worth about 10 percent more than
both rubies and sapphires. Burma and Thailand dump
tons of rubies and sapphires on the world markets

every year. Most of the world's emeralds come from South America and seem to be much rarer.

The four Cs that apply to diamonds are also important to the value of colored gemstones. Color is very important. After all, they are colored gems. The color of gems can be enhanced by heat and chemicals, and this is another good reason not to put too much money into them. As far as clarity goes, it is better to have a few flaws in a colored gem, because this can be an indication of its authenticity. Man-made gems can be made with flaws but generally are not. As far as cut goes, it has the least effect on the gem's value. Most all the colored gems I've seen lately are cut in Asia where the labor is cheap. These are, for the most part, pretty good stones, but I have seen some slop. Carat weight, of course, is also a factor.

How Much to Pay for Colored Gems

Below is a chart that I use to figure what to pay for colored gems. When I refer to the size in points, I mean the points as indicated by my diamond gauge, which is not the actual weight of these stones.

Stone Size	Price Per Stone
1 pt to 5 pts	25 cents to 50 cents per stone
5 pts to 10 pts	50 cents to $1 per stone
10 pts to 25 pts	$1 to $5 per stone
25 pts to 50 pts	$5 to $20 per stone
50 pts and larger	$20 or more per stone

To me, buying these colored gems is like shooting craps. You put your money down, roll the dice, and take your chances. But there is good money to be made if you get a good piece for a low price. If you can buy colored gems at the prices I suggest, it is hard to lose money. For example, I recently purchased an emerald ring that had a large, carat-size, emerald-cut emerald with two triangular-shaped diamonds on each side, and it was mounted in an 18k gold ring. The diamonds tested as real and appeared to weigh about 25 pts together. I figured that I would give the customer about $25 for the diamonds. The 18k gold mounting weighed more than 2 dwt for an additional $15 dollars. The emerald had a nice green color to it and a few small visible flaws. It appeared to be real—I'd seen many man-made emeralds and their color was usually darker—so I added another $35 for the emerald for a total of $75. After keeping the ring for the required number of days, I put it out for sale for $395. Eventually, I sold it to the girl who works for me for $250. She took the ring down the street to a local appraiser, who estimated the ring's value at more than $1,000. Needless to say, she was very happy.

There is good money to be made with these colored gems, but until you have gained experience, be careful. Don't worry about a customer walking away because you made a low offer. Normally, you can buy these pieces for your price, and there will be someone else right behind the customer who walked away who is willing to sell to you.

OTHER STONES

Stones like topaz, pearls, opals, and amethyst are valued mainly for the gold in their mountings or the diamonds around them. You will see the large quartz-type stones like topaz and amethyst mounted in 10k and 14k rings. Some of these stones can be more than an inch wide and quite heavy. These pieces should be purchased mainly for their gold, and the approximate weight of the stone should be deducted. Generally, if the stone is smaller than the largest ring in my diamond gauge, I will not deduct its weight. If it is between that size and the size of a dime, I will deduct 1 or 2 dwt. If the stone is larger than a dime, I will deduct 3 or 4 dwt. For instance, if the ring weighs 10 dwt, and the stone weighs 3 or 4 dwt, you should only pay for 5 or 6 dwt.

If the stones are smaller and look attractive, I will usually count them as part of the gold weight. Or, if the amount I come up with is a dollar or two short of an even number, I will usually add enough to make a round number. For instance, if I have a ring with an opal that weighs enough to give $18, I will usually offer an even $20 if I think I can sell the ring as jewelry.

I always buy these rings at prices that allow a profit if they must be scrapped. If they look nice enough, I will try to sell them first because I can usually get about twice their scrap value this way. Any rings that have a scratched or damaged stone will almost always wind up in the scrap pile.

WATCHES

There are few modern wristwatches that sell well in my pawnshop. Every drug store, grocery store, and discount store in the country sells wristwatches, and the market is flooded with this cheap junk. Men's and ladies' digital and cheap quartz analog watches are very hard to sell. People can buy new watches for as little as $10 that look good and will last for a year.

When their cheap watch stops working, they just go and buy a new one. Because of this, I have stopped taking all but a few select models of watches. Rolex, Seiko, Citizen, and other high-quality models are all that are worth taking.

Rolex watches are always in great demand. I will purchase and make loans on all the good clean Rolexes I can get. I will loan 25 to 30 percent of their new retail price and purchase them for 5 percent more than that if the watch is like new and in the box. Rolexes retail for as much as $12,000 or more. Most of the ones I see are the average stainless-steel models, and I will offer $300 to $400 for a loan on these. If you don't know what Rolexes sell for, go to a local dealer and get a price list. Don't tell him you're a pawnbroker, but ask him what his best cash price would be for both a man's and a lady's mid-range model like a stainless steel Datejust. If he will discount them, and most dealers will, you can adjust the prices on the list by this percentage and have a good idea what a new Rolex costs.

Beware of fake Rolexes. There are a lot of them around. Most fake Rolexes have quartz movements and a hesitating second hand that stops at every second, which gives them away. There are fake Rolexes around with self-winding movements just like the real ones, and the only way to be sure it's a genuine Rolex is to remove the wristband and look for its serial number. Always get the customer's permission before you do this, and make sure you don't scratch or damage the watch. Push a straight pin into the holes on each side of the lugs to compress the spring-loaded pin that attaches the wristband to the watch. There should be numbers stamped in the case on each side where the band was. The number without any letters in it is usually the serial number. The wristband of a real Rolex will also have a number on the underside of the clasp mechanism. If the watch is gold or gold and stainless steel, the number will be marked on the case and the band as 14 or 18 without a "k."

Seiko and Citizen are also good brands, but, unlike Rolexes, they are sold by all the discount stores. Therefore, the catalogs for these stores are good places to reference prices for these watches. I am mainly interested in men's and ladies' sports watches that retail new for more than $150. The Seiko and Citizen diver's and pilot's watches are especially good. I will loan 15 to 25 percent of their new retail price and purchase them for 5 percent more than that if they are like new and in the box.

There are also collectible Swiss and American watches. They are rare, and if you get one that you think might be valuable, it is best to contact one of the watch buyers I list in Appendix C. They will help you evaluate it and may even be interested in buying it from you. Good collectible pocket watches are scarce these days. Ten years ago, there were lots of good vintage pocket watches around, but I'm lucky to see one or two per year now. The value of pocket watches can be hard to determine. Most of them can be pawned or purchased for $25 to $100 and can be sold for double or triple that amount. The best way to test a pocket watch is to have the customer bring it in unwound and not running. When the watch is wound all the way up and starts running, it is a good sign that it works. The fact that it ran well enough to unwind the main spring is proof that it will keep time.

One thing to consider with pocket watches and

wristwatches is if they run and keep time. Unless you are a watchmaker, there are few things you can do short of wearing or carrying the watch. Usually, if a customer comes in wearing a watch and it has the correct time and date on it, then it is probably good. If the time or date is incorrect, beware. Always avoid dirty, beat-up watches with scratched crystals, because people won't buy them. Watches can be very expensive to repair, especially vintage pocket watches. Try to get an estimate before you commit to having one fixed, because some cost more to fix than they are worth. Find a good watchmaker in your area who will fix your watches at dealer's rates.

PREPARING YOUR JEWELRY FOR SALE

After several months in business, you will begin to accumulate a lot of good jewelry to sell. As soon as you open your doors for business and have all the proper licenses to buy and pawn gold, try to get all the jewelry you can to start filling your showcases. Almost all the jewelry you get will need to be cleaned or polished or both. Some of it will need to be repaired. The jewelry supply companies listed in Appendix C carry many books and videos on jewelry repair in their catalogs. Jewelry repair is not absolutely necessary to know, but you should learn how to polish jewelry. Your jewelry will sell much better if it is clean and presented professionally. Many jeweler's schools are also listed in Appendix C.

Cleaning Jewelry
You will need a good buffing machine, sources for which I list in Appendix C. Even if you choose not to buff

your jewelry, you should, at the very least, buy a good ultrasonic cleaning machine. You can buy one of these from the same place you buy all your jewelry tools.

An ultrasonic jewelry cleaner takes more common sense than skill to operate. Just fill it with water and ammonia (I use a 50/50 mixture), turn it on, and put in your jewelry. I recommend you get one with a heated tank. The two main things you should remember about ultrasonic machines is that they can shake mounted stones loose if the stones are not tight, and the harsh ammonia can eat up soft stones like opals and pearls. Unless you are trained to repair jewelry, never put a customer's ring in your ultrasonic machine or try to buff it on your buffing machine. Even though I am a trained goldsmith, I have had accidents using both of these machines. My buffing machine once grabbed a large rope chain I was trying to buff and tore the chain to pieces, beating the hell out of my hand in the process. If the chain had belonged to a customer, I would have had to buy him another one.

Before setting your jewelry out for sale, you should make sure all stones are tight and all the prongs meant to hold them in place are present. If not, get them fixed. Customers get angry when the ring they just bought from you loses a stone the next day. Also make sure all your chains and bracelets have good clasps on them. Basically, all your jewelry should look as close to new as possible.

Repairing Jewelry

I spent six months at Bowman's Academy to learn basic jewelry repair, but there are now several good two-week courses offered in many parts of the country. But the pawnshop business is the perfect place to learn and practice this trade. There will be plenty of broken and damaged jewelry to practice on, and if you screw up, just scrap your mistakes.

I do all jewelry repairs for my pawnshop. When I first opened, I also took in customer jewelry for repair and did ring sizing and mounted stones. This can be an excellent source of extra income for your fledgling business. It also helps to sell your jewelry if people know you are a goldsmith and service the product you sell.

If you can't or don't want to repair jewelry or size rings for customers, find a good goldsmith that will do the work for you at shop prices. You can make extra money by charging your customers a few dollars more than your cost.

Casting Jewelry

A friend of mine who is in the pawnbroking business separated the jewelry part from the rest of one of his pawnshops and now offers a full-service jewelry store in conjunction with his pawnshop business. He rarely scraps his old gold. Instead, he melts it and recasts it into new jewelry. This can be a good way to stock your showcase with jewelry, especially when you are just getting started. Even if you aren't inclined to do the work yourself or don't want to buy all the expensive equipment necessary to cast jewelry, you can usually find someone in your area who will do it for you.

There are also places that will do this kind of work for you by mail. These are listed in Appendix C. One thing to remember to do when having your scrap cast into jewelry is weigh it before you send it, and weigh it when you get it back. Some reduction in weight is

These are my showcases with the jewelry trays spread out for sale.

I make my own trays out of Styrofoam and black felt.

expected, but it should be less than 5 percent. You will also need to give the goldsmith more gold than it will take to actually make the jewelry so there is enough to completely fill the mold. Just make sure he sends back all the leftovers or gives you credit toward his labor.

Displaying Jewelry

The way you display your jewelry can be very helpful to your sales. I try make my jewelry displays as nice as the jewelry stores'. You will need good glass showcases that can be locked. Used showcases are the best deal as long as they are clean and presentable. Two 5- or 6-foot long showcases should be plenty to start with. They should have lights in them. I also use track lights over my showcases with 40-watt spotlights to add sparkle to my diamonds and other gems. They also help highlight the gold jewelry.

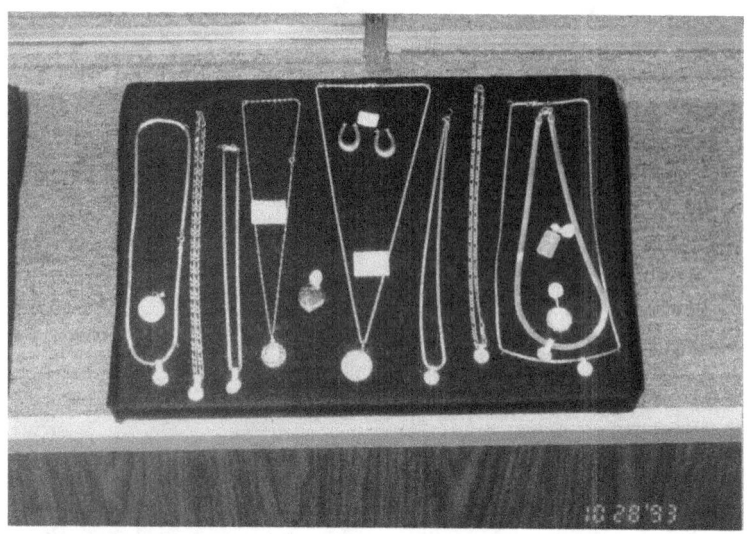

These boards make nice chain and pendant displays. These pieces are pinned to the board with jeweler's U-pins.

These homemade trays stack nicely to be stored in my safe.

It's not necessary to buy all your jewelry displays from expensive wholesalers when you can make most of what you need yourself. Most of my jewelry is displayed on 1-inch-thick 12-by-18-inch Styrofoam boards, which are covered with thick black felt that is stitched or pinned underneath. I have found that black is the best background color to show off gold jewelry.

I use jeweler's U-pins to mount chains and charms for display. The Styrofoam boards are available at your local hobby and craft store, and the U-pins can be purchased from a jewelry supply wholesaler. The black felt is available at any fabric store.

By cutting the Styrofoam boards to fit smaller spaces in the showcase and on the shelves, I can fill my cases with jewelry. When I'm ready to close at night, these boards can be stacked on top of each other and placed into my safe.

I can also rearrange the chains and charms on the trays to make many different and attractive displays. When I put the boards on the bottom shelf of the showcase, I use felt-covered wood blocks to prop them up in the rear, which gives the customer a better look.

To display rings, I use the same size boards for the base, but I place two 2-by-3-by-12-inch felt-covered blocks on the ends of the boards without attaching them. Then I put rows of model 11v black-on-black ring boxes (see B. Rush Apple in Appendix C) on the boards between the blocks with their lids open. At the end of the day, I stack the boards so they fit in the safe. Of course, the board on top won't need the blocks, so I can fit a few extra boxes on it.

I do buy some factory-made ring trays to display some of my best pieces. These trays usually hold a dozen rings and fit nicely on the uppermost shelves without blocking the view of the jewelry below them. When showing the jewelry in these ring trays, I try to take out only one piece at a time. That way, if the customer is actually a thief and runs with my ring, I will only lose one, not a dozen. I also like to use factory-made trays to display earrings and small charms. Some charms are hard to tag and have to be put in compartment trays with a price tag on each compartment. It is also best to show these one at a time, because they are so easy to switch around. You must also be careful when handling these trays, because the charms can be knocked into different compartments, causing you to sell a $50 charm for $5.

When you buy price tags, always get sharkskin-type tags that can't be torn off easily and have to be cut to be removed. Besides tagging each and every piece of jewelry with a sharkskin price tag, I also put price tags on the lids of my ring boxes so they are clearly visible to my customers. The prices on my chains are also shown clearly. I don't understand why some jewelers and pawnbrokers hide the prices on their merchandise, unless they are ashamed or less than honest. I find that when prices are clearly visible, I save time and trouble. My customers can shop my case and see what is in their price range. When I put my jewelry on sale, the customer can see that I've honestly marked the price down. Also, I am proud of the low prices at which I sell my jewelry.

TIPS ON SELLING JEWELRY

1) Always keep your ring trays full because empty trays encourage thieves. If you show a tray of rings with empty spaces to someone, it is hard to prove how many rings were in the tray.

2) Tag all your jewelry, especially your rings, with price tags, because customers can switch boxes if you let them look at more than one piece of jewelry at a time. (It is a good idea to show only one piece at a time.) You can sell a $500 ring for $50 if it is in the wrong box, even if it is tagged.

3) When showing jewelry to a customer, always look carefully at what they hand back to you, especially if the customer is wearing other pieces of jewelry. It is easy to slip a fake in a ring box undetected. If all your jewelry is tagged with hard-to-remove tags, it is easier to foil these scams.

4) Always keep your showcases locked. Some people have long arms with quick hands on the end of them. A whole tray of rings can disappear before you know it.

5) Watch out for grab-and-runners. These people will grab and run as soon as you put a tray of expensive rings near their hands.

6) Christmas is not only a time for giving, it is also a time for stealing.

7) Keep your showcases clean and orderly. People will buy more from a clean display.

8) Have a velvet cloth handy to wipe greasy finger-prints off your nice clean jewelry.

9) Buy a small hand-held or countertop mirror so your customers can try on necklaces and see them on their necks.

10) A small magnifying glass will help your customers get a better look at your jewelry.

11) A sales pitch I use to help sell my jewelry is, "If a GIA-certified appraiser doesn't appraise this piece for at least twice what you paid me for it, I'll refund the difference to make it so."

12) If a customer doubts the authenticity of my dia-monds or gold, I tell them about my modern elec-tronic testing equipment, and, if necessary, I'll test the item while they watch.

6 Guns

Guns are my favorite part of the pawnshop business. I was raised around firearms and I enjoy shooting and collecting them. Firearms can and should be a very profitable part of your pawnshop business. Some of you may already be in the gun business and think you can skip this chapter. I suggest you read it anyway so you can see the gun business the way a pawnbroker does. Those of you who want to be pawnbrokers and don't own or like guns should also read this chapter.

Guns are a form of wealth, and customers may want to pawn them to you. If you don't like the idea of selling guns that come out of pawn to the general public, I recommend wholesaling them to local gun shops. Most gun dealers look for sources to buy good used guns, and they will usually pay a fair price. Thus, you can pawn guns and sell any unredeemed pieces without actually being in the gun business. Personally, I prefer to retail almost all of the firearms I get, because I make a much better profit than if I were to wholesale them.

When I first opened my shop, it was easy to sell all the used guns I got my hands on. But in the last few years,

Virginia has earned a bad (and undeserved) reputation as being an easy place to acquire firearms. The state and federal governments recently passed several laws that have made the gun business more complicated and difficult.

GETTING YOUR FEDERAL FIREARMS LICENSE

The first thing you will need in order to deal in firearms is a Federal Firearms License (FFL), which is issued by the Bureau of Alcohol, Tobacco, and Firearms (BATF). The BATF is a division of the U.S. Treasury Department. They issue a special license for pawnbrokers that costs $90 for three years. (It was only $30 for three years when I started this book.) The BATF requires proof that you have a business license and a place of business. You are also required to provide your fingerprints.

I recommend that you apply for your FFL as soon as possible. Since the political climate in Washington has become so antigun, the process of issuing FFLs has slowed to a crawl, and it may take months for you to get your first license. Virginia and most other states now require that you have state firearms dealers licenses as well. Get your application for these licenses in as soon as possible too.

Do not deal in firearms until you have all the proper licenses. Always obey the letter of the law, because there are many antigun politicians and bureaucrats who will take your licenses away or, even worse, prosecute you if you don't. Once I received a call from an assistant to the state police commissioner who threatened to take my state license because I had failed to check one small box on a form. Incidents like this are rare, and I normally have excellent relations with the authorities, but they demonstrate the need to be extra careful when dealing with guns.

KEEPING GUN RECORDS

Good record keeping is another important aspect of the firearms business. You will need a Firearms Acquisition and Disposition Book or other bound book in which to keep these records. The BATF has specific guidelines for these books. The acquisition side should have spaces to write where or from whom a gun was pawned or purchased. It should also have spaces to write in the manufacturer and/or importer, model, serial number, type of action, gauge or caliber, and date received. The acquisition information should also include the address or FFL number of the person from whom the gun was pawned or purchased or, if the gun was purchased new, the name of the wholesaler. The book I use to list guns that are pawned shows only the person's name, not their address. If their address is needed, I can always look it up in my pawn tickets or on my computer.

The disposition side of the book should show the date the firearm was sold or redeemed, who received it, their address or FFL number, and the serial number for the 4473 form that is filled out by the buyer of the gun. Persons with an FFL don't have to fill out form 4473, but a copy of their current FFL must be kept on file. Everyone else must fill out the form each time they buy a firearm. These forms must be logged into your bound books regularly and kept in files on your business premises so that they are available for inspection by the BATF whenever it wants to look at them.

All these forms and books must be kept for as long as

you are in business, and if you go out of business, you must send them to the BATF in Washington, D.C. You also need to keep these records in good order so you can do firearms traces for the BATF. When police agencies need to trace a firearm, they call the BATF. The BATF has all the production records and serial numbers of all firearms manufactured by or imported into this country. The BATF will call the importer or manufacturer to find out which wholesaler purchased the firearm. Then it will call the wholesaler to find out which retailer bought the gun from that wholesaler. Then it will call the retailer to find out who they sold the gun to. The BATF will sometimes try to track down that person to find out what he did with the gun, but this is usually where the system breaks down. Your main concern is to be able to tell the BATF who received any new guns that you may have sold. I have never been asked to trace a used gun.

The method I use for filing the 4473 forms is simple and easy to learn. When I purchase or pawn used firearms, I take down the necessary information for the bound book from the pawn sheets and log in the firearms by date. New guns are logged in a separate bound book, also in chronological order. After the 4473 forms are filled out by my customers, the serial numbers on the forms are logged in the bound book, and the forms are filed in chronological order. You must assign each 4473 form a serial number in the upper right hand corner. For example, the first form I logged in 1994 was number 194-01. This tells me that it was the first form for the first gun transaction made in 1994. You can use any number scheme you want, but I like to have the year that the transaction occurred coded in the serial number. The forms are separated in file folders by month.

When the BATF calls me to do a trace, it can normally be done right over the phone without delay. They tell me the type of gun, the date I received it, the serial number, and the wholesaler who sent it to me. I quickly look up the gun in the acquisitions section of my bound book by the date I received it. Then I look across the page to the disposition side and make a note of who received it and the serial number for the 4473 form that was filled out. I retrieve the file folder for the appropriate month, look up the form by its serial number, and give the BATF the information it needs about the person who bought the gun.

You may be wondering why I don't use the pawnshop's computer to keep all these tedious gun records. The pawnshop program I use to do business has the capability to do my gun records, but there are several reasons why I don't use it. First of all, I like doing my records on paper, and I can't quite bring myself to trust my computer not to lose my records. Also, I'm used to keeping my gun records the old-fashioned way. If I wanted to use my computer to keep my gun records, I would need to write to the BATF for permission to use the computer program I have, and I would have to buy a wide-carriage printer to print out log sheets. Even then, I would still have to keep separate files for the 4473 forms.

HOW MUCH TO PAY FOR GUNS

What you pay for guns, or anything else, should be determined by what you can sell them for. Regional differences can have an effect on this. For example, on the flat plains and prairies of the western states, high-powered rifles bring premium prices, and in the east where the marshes and tide-waters of the Chesapeake Bay attract duck hunters, shotguns are highly valued. The state of Virginia is divided into areas that are either for shotgun hunting or rifle hunting during deer season. Therefore, a good Remington 1100 shotgun will bring top dollar, while I may have to discount a Winchester 30-06 bolt-action rifle in order to sell it.

If you open your pawnshop in an area that has severe restrictions on handguns or assault rifles, it may be difficult or even impossible for you to sell these types of guns, and you may have to find a gun shop in another area to buy them or take them on consignment. Virginia now has a one-gun-a-month law and requires an instant background check that can take up to 48 hours, thus preventing impulse purchases. Both of these stipulations have reduced my handgun sales. Although people must also get an instant background check when they buy long guns, they can buy as many as they want once they're approved, so my long-gun sales haven't been affected as badly.

To help you figure out what guns are worth, you should acquire gun wholesalers catalogs and several gun price guides. You can get all the catalogs you want by sending a copy of your Federal Firearms License, signed in ink, to these wholesalers. Once they have your license on file, you can order guns, ammunition, and accessories at wholesale prices through the mail. Some of these wholesalers are listed in Appendix D. Following is a list of price guides and publications that are available either directly from these wholesalers or from your local bookstore.

Fjestad, S.P. *Blue Book of Gun Values*. Minneapolis: Blue Book Publications, Inc., (updated yearly).

Flayderman, Norm. *Flayderman's Guide to Antique American Firearms*. Illinois: D.B.I. Books, Inc., (updated every three to four years).

Shotgun News. Nebraska: Snell Publishing Company, (published three times per month).

Wahl, Paul. *Gun Trader's Guide*. New Jersey: Stoeger Publishing Company, (updated yearly).

In determining what a firearm is worth, it is helpful to be familiar with firearms and to be able to assess their condition and detect flaws in their mechanical function. A firearm's condition is a very important factor in determining its value. The *Blue Book of Gun Values* lists gun values according to the percentage of their new condition and has a chapter on grading criteria with color photographs. For example, a Smith and Wesson, model 36, .38-caliber, blue steel revolver with a 2-inch barrel was brought in by a customer to be pawned. As soon as the customer handed it to me, I made sure it was not loaded. This is always the first thing to do when you are handed any firearm. After assuring myself that the weapon was clear, I proceeded to evaluate its condition. I estimated by *Blue Book* standards that it was in about 90-percent new condition. The most current edition of the *Blue Book of Gun Values* listed this gun as worth $165 in 90-percent new condition. I thought this was a little low, because I could easily sell the gun for $200 in this area. If the owner had the original box and paperwork, it could sell for as much as $225. The gun came with a holster, but it was an inexpensive nylon one that didn't add much to the gun's value. Most used firearms that are in 95 percent or better new condition and have their original boxes and papers should sell for close to their wholesale price. This gun would wholesale new for around $265 and retail new for $374. I offered this fellow $100 for a loan and $110 to buy it. He elected to pawn the gun for 30 days. If this weapon had come out of pawn, I could have sold it for enough to make back my principal and interest, plus a tidy profit.

Wear, scratches, and other cosmetic defects can decrease a firearm's value. Scopes, slings, special sights, extra magazines, and other accessories can increase the base value of a firearm. For example, I almost always offer a little more money for a rifle that has a good scope. You can find the retail and wholesale prices for rifle and handgun scopes in the catalogs you receive when you send out your FFL. I normally loan or purchase a scope for about 40 percent of its wholesale price. As a matter of fact, 40 percent of wholesale is a good benchmark for what to offer for most guns and accessories. By keeping your investment near this level, you will be able to sell your guns and accessories at a 100-percent markup and still beat the price of the discount stores that sell new guns and accessories for near wholesale prices. For example, a Remington 700 BDL .30-06 bolt-action rifle with a Redfield 3 x 9 scope will wholesale for around $500. Your local Kmart may sell the same rifle for $525 to $550 at retail. I estimate that this rifle, used but in excellent condition, will sell for about $450, which is approximately 80 percent of the price of a new one at Kmart. A good loan would be $150 to $200, and I'd offer around $225 to purchase it. Of course, if there are accessories included, like a case, sling, or ammo, you might want to pay more.

The closer you get to investing half of the value of the firearm, the more you need to be sure that the gun is in its best condition. For instance, you loan $150 on a firearm that you think will sell for $450, and when it comes out of pawn, you discover that it needs repairs. You could spend up to $300 on repairs and just break even. Of course, a $450 firearm that needs $300 worth of repairs should be obvious even to a novice pawnbroker.

DISPLAYING FIREARMS FOR SALE

Once you have acquired some firearms to sell, you should consider how to display them to their best advantage. I display my handguns in locked glass show-cases that I line with red felt. The red felt highlights the guns and gives their presentation a museum-like quality. If a gun came with its box, I will display the gun on top of the closed box to show that it is like new. If it doesn't have a box, I will put it on top of a zipper pouch, supplies of which I buy for this purpose, and include its cost in the price of the handgun. I will also include an extra magazine if the gun came with one. Wiping the guns down with oil gives them a nice shine. All these things help make the guns look as new as possible so I can get the best possible price for them.

On my price tags, which are always plainly visible, I list the features of the gun and the accessories that come with it along with the price. All the used guns you put out for sale should be clean and in good shooting condition. I will sometimes test-fire a gun if I think it might not work properly. Since I don't give warranties

I display my handguns in locked glass showcases lined with red felt.

on the used guns I sell, I will sometimes test-fire a gun for a customer to show him that it works. I keep a 55-gallon drum in the back of my shop for this purpose. It is filled about three quarters with fine sand and placed on its side on top of sandbags. There are also sandbags piled around it and on top of it. Stand back a few feet before shooting into it so the dust and sand doesn't blow back all over you and the firearm. Make sure the weapon is pointed at the center of the barrel so the bullets stay inside of it. I once shot a friend's M11 machine gun in this barrel and it climbed out of the center and put a few rounds in the wall. I have shot everything from high-powered rifles to shotguns in this barrel and never had any problems as long as I kept the gun pointed at the center of the barrel.

Since most rifles and shotguns are too long to fit in glass showcases, I display them horizontally on Peg-Board walls behind the handgun cases. Keeping the rifles and shotguns behind the counter enables my customers to see them but prevents them from handling the guns unless I show one to them. This keeps the guns from getting new scratches or scars and keeps me from having to wipe off fingerprints. Some pawnshop and gun shop owners display their guns in racks on the showroom floor and allow customers to handle them. I would always worry that some idiot was going to take a round from his pocket, load a gun, and use it to rob me or injure himself or someone else in my store. That would result in a terrible lawsuit.

Ammunition is an item that you should keep in stock. There is a limited profit potential in ammunition, but it pays to keep some on hand. I sell it, use some to test-fire guns, and shoot some myself for recreational purposes. But I'm lucky if I get a 20- or 30-percent markup on it.

I display my rifles and shotguns horizontally on pegboard walls out of customers' reach.

There was a shake-up in the ammunition business recently when Congress discussed increasing the tax on ammo in conjunction with the health care bill. Also, the President recently banned all arms and munitions manufactured in China, which cut off a steady supply of cheap and popular ammo. These two acts caused prices to go up and supplies to go down. In addition, the BATF decided arbitrarily that some of the rifle ammo that had been imported (7.62 x 39) was armor-piercing handgun ammo and prohibited it from being sold to the public. People who had already bought some of the ammo were told to either shoot it up themselves or sell it to police departments. Also, there was a rumor going around among gun owners that the government had a secret pact with the ammunition manufacturers to develop a primer that would disintegrate, thereby giving ammo a limited shelf life. Consequently, people bought all the ammo they could afford, so supplies of most ammo were limited for a while but have returned to normal.

Before you stock too much ammo, check the prices and brands available at your local Kmart so you know what you're up against. These places will sometimes use ammo as a "loss leader" to get customers in their stores to buy other things. They sometimes sell their ammo at retail for less than what you can order it for at wholesale. I always buy their .22-caliber ammo when they put it on sale. I buy 10 or 20 boxes at 90 cents or $1 per box and sell it for $1.50 per box. If my customers want to buy .22-caliber. ammo for a gun they just bought in my store, it is more convenient for them to buy it from me than go somewhere else to save 50 cents. Don't try to stock a wide variety of ammo; just stock what you need for the guns you have on hand and for your personal use.

HOW TO EVALUATE FIREARMS

If you are unfamiliar with firearms but you wish to have them in your pawnshop, then it is in your best interest to learn all you can about them. I can explain the basics to you here, but you will need to read other books, take some firearms safety or self-defense courses, and do some shooting. Guns are machines and therefore can be evaluated by how well they function as well as by their cosmetic appearance. If a firearm shows abuse in its outside appearance, it may also have been abused mechanically.

Whenever a customer hands you a firearm to evaluate, you should immediately determine whether it is loaded. In fact, it is best to handle it as though it is loaded. It should always be pointed in a safe direction and your finger kept off the trigger.

Revolvers

Revolvers have been around since the mid 1800s, and it was Col. Sam Colt who first perfected their design. Except for the change in ammunition from black powder cap and ball to smokeless powder with metallic cartridges, they have basically remained unchanged.

There are two categories of revolvers to consider: single-actions and double-actions. The single-action revolver works by first manually cocking the hammer, which causes the cylinder to rotate and line up a cartridge in front of the barrel. When the trigger is pulled, the firing pin strikes the cartridge and fires it. The hammer must be cocked again to repeat this process. To unload the single-action revolver, you must open the loading gate, a trap door on the right side of the weapon. Newer single-actions will free the cylinder so it can be rotated when the trap door is opened. The spring-loaded rod under the barrel will help you push the cartridges out of the cylinder. Older single-actions must have their hammers half-cocked to free their cylinders. With your finger off the trigger, cock the hammer until you can spin the cylinder freely. After the weapon is clear, cock the hammer all the way and release it by pulling the trigger and lowering the hammer with your thumb until the hammer rests against the frame.

To check the proper functioning of the revolver, continue to hold the trigger against the frame. This is the position the revolver is in at the moment of firing. With your free hand, twist the cylinder back and forth. It shouldn't move at all, and if it moves more than about 1/16 inch, it could be unsafe to shoot. While still holding the weapon in this position, check to see if the firing pin is poking through the frame behind the cylinder chamber that is lined up with the barrel. If it isn't, then the firing pin could be broken. This applies only to older single-actions, as the firing pins on newer single-actions are not visible.

Double-action revolvers work on the same principle as single-action revolvers. The "double action" designation refers to the difference in the way the weapon is fired. Double-actions can be fired two ways: by cocking the hammer manually then pulling the trigger or by merely pulling the trigger, which automatically cocks the hammer and releases it. To unload the double-action revolver, the cylinder release button must be pushed to release the cylinder, which swings out to the left. There is a rod in the front of the cylinder that, when pushed toward you, will eject all the cartridges in the cylinder at once. There are some double-actions that unload like single-actions, and there are also break-top revolvers that have frames that are hinged in the middle. These usually have releases near the hammer, and as they are broken open, the cartridges are automatically ejected out of the cylinder.

You should check all double-action revolvers for proper functioning using the previously described method. Also, the barrels of revolvers should be checked for bulges and obstructions. Check for cracks in the frame or cylinder, broken parts, and missing screws. Don't confuse the side plates on some revolvers for cracks in the frame. The stocks (grips) should be without chips or cracks. If the weapon has adjustable sights, they should be in good condition.

The metal finish of the revolver can make a big difference in its value. The types of finishes you will mostly see are blue, nickel, and stainless steel. Stainless steel is actually not a finish but the natural color of the steel used to make the gun. As such, it is the most desirable because it can't wear off. Nickel and blue finishes can wear off.

Do not reject outright every revolver that isn't perfect. If a revolver is in good mechanical condition but has poor cosmetic appearance, it can still be profitable. I pay much less for ugly guns and either sell them as is or send them out to be refinished. Even guns that have mechanical problems can be profitable if you pay as little as possible for them. Don't miss out on a profit just because a gun isn't perfect. For instance, old Colt single-actions bring hundreds of dollars even if they have no finish, won't shoot, and have missing parts.

Semiautomatic Handguns

Semiautomatic handguns were perfected around the turn of the century by John Browning and others. This type of handgun has gained much popularity since then because of its increased firepower. Every armed force in the world issues its troops semiautomatic handguns, and nearly every police department in this country has replaced its antiquated revolvers with them.

Semiautomatics work by first inserting a loaded magazine into the weapon and pulling backward on the slide (or bolt). This strips a cartridge off the top of the magazine and feeds it into the barrel. The action of the slide also cocks the hammer of the gun, making the weapon ready to fire. Pulling the trigger causes the hammer to hit the firing pin, which discharges the cartridge. The gun automatically ejects the empty case, cocks the hammer again, and feeds the next cartridge into the barrel, making it ready to fire again immediately. What makes the gun semiautomatic is that the trigger must be pulled one time for each round fired. Any weapon that fires repeatedly when the trigger is held down is an automatic weapon and is either illegal or severely restricted.

Most semiautomatics have safeties, which prevent the weapon from accidentally discharging. Some safeties are engaged automatically when the first round is chambered, and others must be engaged manually. When a customer hands you a semiauto to evaluate, you should clear it immediately. With the weapon pointed in a safe direction and your finger off the trigger, remove the magazine. Some guns have the magazine releases on the grip next to the trigger, while others have them on the bottom of the grip. If the gun's magazine release is not on the grip, look for it near your thumb as you grab the magazine with your left hand. Pull back the slide (bolt), and any cartridges in the barrel will be ejected. Then look into the chamber of the barrel to make sure it is empty. Most accidents with semiautos happen when the slide is pulled back to eject the round in the chamber and clear the weapon without removing the magazine first. The person then removes the magazine thinking he has cleared the weapon, when he has really fed a round into the barrel. I wish I had a dollar for every gun that's been handed to me that was cleared this way. I have even done it myself and seen friends do it who should know better.

You will see the same finishes that are on revolvers on semiautos. Again, stainless steel is the most desirable. Blue and nickel finishes are also desirable but are worth slightly less. You should check all semiautos for cracks in their frames and slides. The stocks should not be cracked or chipped, and all screws should be present. Check the empty weapon for proper functioning by cycling the slide, putting on the safety if the gun has one, and trying to pull the trigger. If the hammer doesn't fall, and if the weapon has a hammer you can get your thumb on, lower it gently to decock the gun. Some semiautos have manual safeties that automatically decock the hammer. If a gun is so equipped, make use of it.

Semiautos should be slightly loose to function properly, but if the gun rattles when you shake it, it is too loose. Look at the bearing surfaces where the slide and frame meet. If there appears to be an inordinate amount of looseness or signs of wear, you may have a gun that is only good for its parts. The sights should also be tight and have all parts present. Test-firing is the only way to prove that a semiauto actually functions properly. When I have any doubt about one of these guns, I will take it to my test-firing barrel, load it up, and fire it. I will usually only put three or four rounds in it just in case it is worn enough to go full auto.

Appropriate magazines are critical to the proper functioning of a semiauto. The magazines should fit properly. Examine them carefully for bent lips on top. There should be at least one magazine with the gun but preferably more. An original magazine is the most desirable—replacement magazines can be expensive and hard to obtain. The magazine for a rare gun can cost $150 or more. I deduct at least 25 percent for missing or damaged magazines.

Rifles

The BATF defines a rifle as "any weapon designed to be fired from the shoulder and made to use the energy of the explosive in a fixed metallic cartridge to fire only a single projectile through a rifled bore for each single pull of the trigger." Rifles must have a minimum 16-inch barrel and be at least 26 inches long. As with all firearms, always unload and clear any rifle before evaluating it.

Here are some of the rifles you may encounter in your pawnshop: single-shot, double-barrel, and combination (rifle and shotgun), bolt-action, pump-action, lever-action, and semiauto. Single-shots, double-barrels, and combinations are the least encountered kinds of rifles. They usually have a button or lever near the top of the pistol grip portion of the stock that breaks the rifle open when pressed. There are other styles, like rolling blocks and trap-door actions, that must have their hammers cocked before they can be opened.

Single-shots should have tight actions, stocks without cracks, working safeties, and good rifling—spiral grooves inside the barrel that make the bullet spin. Rifling is very important to all rifles, because accuracy is the main reason to carry a rifle. If a rifle barrel is damaged or the rifling inside is worn, the rifle isn't good for anything but parts.

Bolt-action rifles are opened by pulling up and back on the bolt. You may have to put the safety in the "off" position to open the bolt. When a bolt-action is opened, the bolt should feel somewhat loose, but when closed, it shouldn't be loose at all. Bolt-actions can be single shot, but most are magazine fed. Some have magazines that are removable, while others have built-in magazines. Always empty the magazines before closing the bolt. With most bolt-actions, holding down the trigger will decock the gun as the bolt is closed. Check the barrel, sights, and stock, and make sure all screws and other parts are present. Also check the safety.

Pump-actions work by pulling the front forearm of the rifle toward the rear of the rifle. There is a release button, usually near the trigger, which will unlock the action so this can be accomplished. Most pump-actions will have a magazine that should be removed before the action is worked. There are a few pump-action rifles that have tubular magazines and must be cleared by holding down the release and working the action. Once you've cleared the gun, close it back up. The action should lock up tightly. Put the safety in the "on" position and pull the trigger. If the safety holds, take it off, pull the trigger, and see if the action releases when the hammer falls. Check the rifling, stocks, sights, and other components as previously described.

Lever-action rifles work by pushing down and forward on the lever, which opens the bolt and cocks the hammer. Most lever-action rifles have tubular magazines attached under the barrel, but a few have detachable magazines. If the magazine can be removed, remove it before working the lever. Sometimes the lever may feel a little loose when it is fully opened. This is normal for most guns, especially Winchesters. You cannot pull the trigger until the lever is pulled up tight against the frame and the bolt is fully closed. This safety feature prevents the gun from firing before the bolt is fully closed.

Semiautomatic rifles work basically the same as semiauto handguns. Although most have detachable magazines, some are tube-fed, and others, like the M1 Garand, have stripper clips. Remove the magazine, if possible, before opening up the weapon to clear the barrel. Some tube-fed rifles can only be cleared by working their bolts to feed and eject any cartridges in the magazine. They should come with at least one good serviceable magazine.

Shotguns

The BATF defines a shotgun as "a weapon designed to be fired from the shoulder and made to use the energy of the explosive in a fixed shotgun shell to fire either a number of ball shot or a single projectile through a smooth bore for each single pull of the trigger." All shotguns must be at least 26 inches long and have barrels no shorter than 18 inches. Break-open, pump-action, bolt-action, and semiauto are the most common types of shotguns.

Break-open shotguns include single-barrel, double-barrel, and over-under. They are all checked in the same manner. There is a lever near your thumb or trigger finger when the gun is held in the firing position that will break open the weapon when pressed. Open the action and clear the barrel(s). The fit between the barrel and receiver should be tight. The forearm (normally wood) should fit tight, be without cracks, and have all the necessary hardware. The forearm and its hardware are what holds the gun together when it is broken open. A cracked wooden forearm can be very expensive to replace. Also look for cracks in the pistol grip area of the buttstock. This is a weak point, especially for double-barrel guns with two triggers. People will pull both triggers simultaneously, causing recoil that can crack the stock. The barrels should be smooth and shiny inside. Pits and dents can be removed by a gunsmith, but this is an added expense. Bulges in barrels are irreparable and dangerous. Guns with bulges are good only for parts. Beware of old shotguns with damascus barrels. These guns were made to fire black powder shotgun shells, and, unless extremely rare, they are good only as wall hangings.

Many break-open guns have a finish on their receivers called color case hardening. This finish is difficult and expensive to replace. The blued finish on double-barrel and over-under guns is also difficult and expensive to replace. The barrels on these guns are soldered together, and the process of bluing involves dipping the parts in heated vats of chemicals that melt the solder. Some of these guns can have five-figure values, which are often estimated by the amount of original finish remaining. The ***Blue Book of Gun Values*** not only lists values by percentage of original finish but other features such as these that add value to rifles.

I like to keep some fired shotgun shells handy to test the firing pins on these guns. I put a small piece of masking tape over the cap, put it in the gun, and pull the trigger to see if the pins are striking it. This a good way to check other shotguns' firing pins as well. Always put on the safety before pulling the trigger to make sure it works. It is not a good idea to dry-fire break-open guns, especially old ones, because their hardened firing pins have a tendency to break if they don't have a shotgun shell to stop their forward momentum.

Pump-action, bolt-action, and semiauto shotguns, for the most part, function the same as rifles with the same style actions. Most pump-action and semiauto shotguns will have to have their actions cycled by hand to empty them, as few of them have detachable magazines.

Antique and Black Powder Guns

Nearly every black powder gun ever manufactured is currently being reproduced. There are vast differences between the values of the originals and the reproductions. Most reproductions are easy to identify by their markings and manufacturers, but there are fakes around that will even fool experts. I recommend using *Flayderman's Guide to Antique American Firearms* to help identify any antique pieces that you may encounter.

Muzzle-loaded rifles and black powder revolvers are much harder to unload than cartridge guns. With muzzle-loaders, you must first determine if the piece is loaded. This can be done with the ramrod, if the ramrod is the original length, by inserting it into the barrel, keeping the muzzle pointed away from your face. If the piece is unloaded, the ramrod should stick out of the barrel just enough so you can pull it back out. Make sure there is not a live cap under the hammer or powder in the flash pan when you are doing this. If the ramrod sticks out far enough for you to wrap your entire hand around it, then it may be loaded. The best way to unload these guns is to fire them. Although you could fire it into your test-firing barrel, the discharge of black powder indoors will make enough smoke to set off every smoke detector in your building. If you can't fire it outdoors, it is best to let the customer take the weapon home and fire it himself. It is not safe to have loaded black powder guns in storage or for sale, and if you can't take it unloaded, don't take it.

It's easier to see if black powder revolvers are loaded because the lead balls are visible in the cylinders. The best way to unload these is also by firing the gun. Black powder guns should be checked for defects just like their modern counterparts. Rust, corrosion, and pitting inside and out are especially bad problems with these guns, because black powder is highly corrosive. If the owner doesn't thoroughly wash and oil his gun after each shooting using black powder or Pyrodex (black powder substitute), it can become a worthless piece of iron very quickly.

Recently, there has been a resurgence in the popularity of black powder firearms, especially the muzzle-loaded hunting rifle. Many states now have special black-powder-gun hunting seasons. I pawn many more of these rifles now than I did just a few years ago. These guns can be sold through the mail unrestricted, and no paperwork is necessary for their transfer. Many discount houses and mail-order catalogs discount these guns at or below the wholesale prices distributors sell them for. Used muzzle-loaders sell for about 60 to 80 percent of their new wholesale price.

Air Guns

Air guns are increasing in popularity these days as the government increases restrictions on regular firearms. There are many backyards in America where air rifles and pistols can be fired legally but firearms can't. Air guns have been popular in Europe for years because of their extremely restrictive gun laws, and some of the most expensive and sophisticated air guns come from that part of the world. Some of these guns cost thousands of dollars new.

I depend on my firearms distributors catalogs to value these pieces. Like black powder guns, air guns require no licenses or paperwork to buy and sell, and they can also be sold through the mail. Used air rifles bring about the same 60 to 80 percent of their wholesale price that black powder guns do. Air rifles are easy to test-fire, because a thick phone book will absorb just about any projectile fired from them. I like to keep a small supply of .177- and .22-caliber pellets on hand to check the functioning of these guns. If you open the gun and there is no pellet in the chamber, it is best to cock and load the gun, then test-fire it. Dry-firing these guns can damage their mechanisms.

TIPS ON SELLING GUNS

1) When showing a buyer a gun, always open the action to make sure it is unloaded before handing

Waiver of Responsibility

    I,_____,am buying this
firearm for myself and I have complied with all laws governing purchase and possession
thereof.I am aware of the proper procedures and methods for the safe handling and maintenance
of this and all other firearms.I realize that all firearms are dangerous and can cause
damage to property, death or bodily injury to myself or other persons and their use or misuse
may have legal ramifications which cause litigation or my personal incarceration.Therefore
I release Alexander's Pawn Shop, Alexander's American Pawn Co.,Victor A. Cullen Jr., his
family, agents and employees of any liability or responsibility for anything that occurs
as a result of the purchase, possession, use or misuse of this firearm or any other firearm
previously acquired .I also accept full responsibility for any accident, death,bodily injury
and/or crime committed by persons who have possession of my firearms even if they have
possession illegally or without my knowledge or permission. I further understand that all
used firearms are "as is" and that no warranties as to their safe function or operation
are expressed or implied. I hereby certify, by my signature below, that I have read and
understand the above waiver.

        Signed _____

        Date:_____,19____

<u>Safety</u> and <u>Laws</u> information <u>is</u> available.

Statement of Residency

    I certify that I am presently a resident in the state of Virginia or
I am on active duty in the Armed Forces of United States of America and have been per-
manently assigned to this state..

        Signed _____

ALEXANDERS PAWN SHOP
Victor A Cullen, Jr.
2715 Route 17
YORKTOWN VIRGINIA 23693
(804) 257 8733
FFL # 8 54 097 02 1B 20369

*I have all gun buyers sign this waiver of responsibility before I
will sell them a gun.*

it to him. Customers have been known to load a
gun without the knowledge of the dealer. When the
next customer looks at the weapon, he could shoot
himself, someone else, or you.

2) Every time I sell a gun, I have the customer sign a waiver of responsibility. With the proliferation of lawsuits against gun dealers and manufacturers, a waiver that is signed and dated by the gun buyer may keep you or your business from being sued into bankruptcy. I will not sell a gun to anyone who will not sign one of these waivers.

3) Broken guns can be sold to parts dealers, but don't expect to get much money. There are listings for these buyers in *Shotgun News*, the largest of which is Gun Parts Corporation of New York (see Appendix D). Gun Parts Corp. also sells an excellent catalog with schematic drawings and parts lists for hundreds of modern and antique firearms.

4) Gun shows can be an excellent way to dispose of any extra firearms. I like to take mine to a show that occurs just before hunting season starts. These shows are also a good place to sell other items, like binoculars, scopes, cameras, ammo, knives, and jewelry.

Work Cited

U.S. Treasury Department. Bureau of Alcohol, Tobacco, and Firearms. *Your Guide to Federal Firearms Regulations*. Washington: Government Printing Office, 1988.

7 Other Merchandise

The variety of merchandise you can buy and pawn in your pawnshop is unlimited. Just about everything you ever wanted, and a lot of things you don't want, will be offered to you. For example, I once pawned a stuffed monkey and a mounted toucan bird for a local taxidermist. Both of them came out of pawn and eventually sold for a profit. Although you may want to acquire oddball items like these for that unique pawnshop "mystique," some items are better than others, and some things should be avoided entirely. While it is impossible to cover everything people will want to pawn, this chapter offers an alphabetical listing of the most common categories of other merchandise that you are likely to encounter.

APPLIANCES

I limit the number and type of home appliances that I take into pawn or buy. Mainly, I deal with microwaves, vacuum cleaners, and small bar-type refrigerators. These appliances are easy to pick up and carry, store on the shelf, and put out for sale. I like to have at least one microwave for sale in my showroom and one in pawn in my storeroom. I have a small microwave, a coffeemaker, and small refrigerator in the rear of my store for my employees and me to use. They were all acquired inexpensively in my pawnshop. All the vacuum cleaners I own were also acquired for dimes on their retail dollar value in my shop. At home I have a Shop Vac, a good quality vacuum cleaner for downstairs, and a good one for upstairs, and I keep a good vacuum at the shop too. They never get to the point of being old or worn out, because they are replaced by newer models as they come into the shop. I have become very selective about what I take in this line, because I could easily become overstocked with these items. You will find that almost any appliance you ever dreamed of will eventually show up in your pawnshop.

The correct functioning of appliances is easy to check. Simply plug them in and try them out. Vacuum cleaners should suck dirt, microwaves should boil a small cup of water in two minutes, and refrigerators should start getting cold in about 10 minutes. People will normally pawn or sell you these items at 10 to 25 percent of their retail price. The most I will pay is 25 percent, and the item must be new in the box for me to do so. The retail cost of an item can usually be determined by looking up the item or a similar one in a discount department store catalog, several of which should be kept on hand. I don't take large appliances in my store unless I need one for my personal use. Large appliances are hard to handle, hard to check out, and they take up a lot of space.

AUTOMOTIVE PARTS AND VEHICLES

I have been in pawnshops that look like junkyards. They have sunroofs, tires, wheels, engine parts, and more. If you are already in the auto-wrecking business, then pawning items like these is great. Otherwise, my advice is to pass on most of this kind of merchandise. I will, on occasion, buy tires, batteries, car stereos, or CB radios for my own use. I tried buying these items for resale at one time and found that many of them had been stolen or didn't work correctly. Car stereos and CB radios are very difficult to check thoroughly, and I won't take the time necessary to do it unless I need the item for my own use. When I do buy these items, the customer must be willing to sell them very cheaply. I will pay 10 cents on the dollar or less, if possible.

The best merchandise to pawn or buy in the automotive category is the automobile itself. I also take motorcycles, trailers, motorhomes, boats, or any other titled vehicle. I have made good profits on these items. Recently, I sold a 1988 Pontiac Grand Prix for $3,000 and realized a $1,500 profit. This car was originally pawned to me, and the owner paid interest on it for several months. He later decided that he could not afford to keep the vehicle and sold it to me. The original loan was $750, and I paid him another $600 to buy it. It needed a new inspection sticker, a little cleaning, and some other work, which came to about $150, so my total investment was only $1,500.

I will take any vehicle in pawn as long as it has a current Virginia state inspection sticker, is legally registered, and has been driven regularly. It must also have a clear title, which must be signed by the owner, leaving any other spaces blank, and left with me while the vehicle is in pawn. I explain to the customer that he is not actually selling the vehicle, and when he pays back the loan and other charges, the title and the vehicle will be returned. Of course, I must take possession of the vehicle and store it in my fenced-in security area at the rear of my shop. Never let the borrower drive the vehicle while you hold the title to it, even if you have a recorded lien against it. It will be much too difficult to take possession of the vehicle if the borrower defaults on the loan. If the borrower does default, you can either have the title changed into your name before selling it, or you can sell the vehicle and let the new owner change the title. Either way, you will have total control.

To determine how much to loan on a vehicle, I keep several used-car Blue Books and pricing guides on hand. These books are available in almost any good bookstore. I value most vehicles at the low end of the scale in the price guides. For example, if the Blue Book lists a vehicle as being worth $1,000, I will loan $300 to $400 for it. If the loan is defaulted, I will be able to take care of any necessary repairs, state inspections, title changes, or other unforeseen difficulties and still be able to make a nice profit. I always check any vehicles I take in pawn as though I were going to buy them for myself. I mostly take only newer model vehicles with average mileage for their age, but I will take older vintage and collectible models if they can be driven legally.

Always secure any vehicles as best you can. I park all the vehicles I pawn in an area that has a 6-foot-high chain-link fence and is well lit, and I put The Club antitheft device on the steering wheel. If you don't have a secured area in which to store vehicles, remove a vital part, such as a distributor rotor, to disable them. If you take in motorcycles, they should be kept indoors if possible.

Trailers can be chained to something, or one wheel can be removed. It is not impossible for the owner to drive away the car he just pawned and go to the Department of Motor Vehicles to replace the title he left with you. These precautions will also help keep thieves from stealing your pledges.

BICYCLES

Buying and pawning used bicycles can be a profitable enterprise if you are careful. The discount stores of America have flooded the country with cheap bikes made in Asia. You can buy all kinds of nice bikes in these stores for less than $150, but most of them are worth less than $100. If you can buy these types of bikes from your customers for $10 to $30, then you can usually make a profit on them. But if you take them in pawn, the small amount of interest you make just barely compensates you for the space they can take up.

The best bikes to take in pawn are the high quality mountain bikes that are so popular. I will even buy cheap mountain bikes, but I avoid the old-style 10 speeds and small children's bikes. The quality mountain bikes can sell for thousands of dollars, but the ones I usually see are in the $200 to $500 range. I will give a loan or buy these bikes for 10 to 25 percent of their new retail cost and sell them for half of their retail cost. You can use the discount department store catalogs to price the cheap bikes, but you may have to visit some bike shops to find catalogs or price sheets for the more expensive bikes.

BOATS

Most boats, especially boats on trailers, are titled vehicles and are similar to automobiles as far as how you should deal with them. I have little experience with large boats, but I will only take one if it has a trailer so I can park it in my lot. It also has to have a clear title signed by the owner. I have also taken many canoes and johnboats, which sell well in the spring. These small unpowered boats do not need titles to be bought and sold. If the customer wants to sell the boat, keep your investment at about half of the price you can sell it for in your store. You should offer about 10 percent less than this price if it is to be pawned.

Boat motors can be hard to check out. I keep a 12-volt converter handy to check electric motors. Small outboard motors that can be picked up can be checked by placing them in a 55-gallon drum of water and letting them run. I always insist that the owner bring in a gas tank with some gas in it for this purpose. Larger motors and inboard-type motors are much more difficult to check. I recommend you take newer motors (less than five years old) and keep your investment at 10 or 20 percent of their potential resale. Boat engines cost two or three times more to be repaired than automobile engines.

Boats and motors are seasonal items, and sometimes people will try to pawn them for small amounts so they can get cheap storage. If you suspect this is the case, you should charge an extra fee for storing these or any other large items. Be reasonable, but don't store large items for the cost of a $10 loan.

There are some price guides for used boats like there are for used cars, but I don't keep one because I don't take that many boats in pawn. Sears puts out a specialty catalog for these items, which can be obtained free-of-charge directly from them.

CLOTHING

Most pawnshops haven't taken clothing in pawn since the Great Depression. Back then, a man would pawn his best Sunday suit on Monday. He would come back on Friday (payday) so he could wear it Saturday night and Sunday to go to meeting. Nowadays there isn't much future in the used clothing business. I have bought some leather motorcycle jackets and made small profits on them, and I do buy some military clothing if I can use it myself. Some pawnshops that are located near military bases will buy uniforms and military outerwear to wholesale to military surplus stores. Collectors will buy antique clothing and old military uniforms, especially the ones with insignia on them. Some pawnbrokers will accept furs in pawn, but unless you have expertise as a furrier and have a cold-storage facility, I don't recommend doing this. You'd also have to watch out for animal rights nuts.

COINS

Coins can be a very profitable part of the pawn-broking business. In my pawnshop, an entire show-case is devoted to a display of coins. I have everything from mint sets to culls for sale. A cull is a coin that is good only for its silver value. These coins are usually severely worn, but you will still be able to recognize them as U.S. coins. They may even have dates that are readable. These coins are traded in commodity markets by the bag and the half bag. A bag contains $1,000 face value worth of U.S. mint pre-1965 silver coins. They can be mixed denominations or of one denomination. Although most of the coins I see are culls, I do get some nice collector's pieces, mint sets, slabs, and complete collections.

It takes years of study and practice to become a certified numismatist who can professionally grade coins, and I cannot tell you everything about coins in this chapter. I can give you a few basics, but if you are not knowledgeable about this subject, it would be in your best interest to learn more.

There are two ways to value coins. One is by their silver value, and the other is by their collector value. Try to make loans or buy coins based on their silver content only. If the coins you are dealing with are of better grades, then you must figure out the collector value, which means you must grade them to the best of your ability. One of the books I use is the **Handbook of United States Coins** by R.S. Yeoman, which lists dealer's buying prices. This and every good coin book has a section on how to grade coins. I find myself reading this section every time I look up a coin to refresh my memory. Most of the values are based not only on the amount of wear to the high points of the coin, but also on its date, where it was minted, and the number of coins minted in that batch. I see very few coins that are uncirculated, and most are valued at the lower to middle end of the scale. I will show customers the value of their coins listed in this book and offer them half of that for a loan and 10 percent more to buy them.

There is also a chart in the back of Yeoman's book that shows the bullion value for each type of coin. Using this chart, you can figure out the silver value for any U.S. coin. For example, if the spot price of silver is $4 per ounce, a pre-1965 silver half-dollar, which has about 1/3 ounce of silver in it, would be worth $1.45. I would offer $1 per coin on a loan and $1.10 per coin to buy them. Most coin dealers will buy these coins for 15 percent less than their silver value and sell them for 15 percent more than their silver value. I like to get them for a little less than 15 percent and sell them for a little more than 15 percent.

Notice that I haven't said much about nonsilver coins, like pennies and nickels. The reason is that there is only a collector's market for these coins. Most Lincoln-head pennies and Jefferson nickels, except for a few rare series, are worth little more than 1 cent and 5 cents, respectively. Most coin dealers will sell Lincoln-head wheat pennies by the roll for slightly more than face value, and most Jefferson nickels end up in my cash register change drawer.

Appendix E lists coin buyers, but be prepared for your coins to be graded lower than you expect and get priced accordingly. When I sell coins, I always try to retail them in my showcase. I use a retail price book like the **Official Blackbook Price Guide**, which is available at your local bookstore, or the Littleton Coin Company's catalog.

ELECTRONIC EQUIPMENT

Almost every home in America has some kind electronic gadget that can be brought to your pawnshop as collateral for a loan or for you to buy. I don't know anyone who doesn't have a television, a videocassette recorder, a stereo, or at least a radio. Electronic equipment is an excellent profit maker for my pawn shop, but what most people don't know is that nothing devalues faster than this equipment. A piece of electronic equipment that is only eight or ten years old may be nearly worthless, even though it works perfectly.

Most electronics manufacturers use what is known as "planned obsolescence" in the design of their products. This means that their products are designed to wear out in five to ten years of normal use. They also try to introduce new technologies at regular intervals so everything they built earlier becomes antiquated and obsolete. Remember eight-track tapes? Cassette tapes made the eight-tracks obsolete. After a while, people with eight-track tape systems couldn't give them away. Compact disks and laser disk players have almost totally replaced LP record albums and the turntables that play them. Soon, digital audiotapes will make CDs and cassettes obsolete. This cycle never ends, and a modern pawnbroker must keep up with new advances in technology.

It is my policy not to take obsolete and outdated electronic equipment, and it should be yours too. Unless my inventory is really low, I won't take electronic equipment that is more than five or six years old. It is not possible to find out the age of every piece of electronic equipment, but some of them are marked with a date of manufacture. Televisions have been required by law since the mid-1970s to be marked with their date of manufacture. Other items can be dated in one of the Orion Blue Books listed in Appendix E. One indication of a piece's age is if it is painted silver. Nearly all stereo and other electronic equipment has been painted black for the last 10 years.

Every piece of electronic equipment that you take in

pawn or purchase should be thoroughly checked out both before you take it in and before you sell it. Unless you can repair these items yourself, the repair cost can cost more than some of these pieces are worth. There should be an area in your store set up as a test bench where all this equipment can be tested quickly and easily. I have a counter in my store that is 36 inches high, 5 feet long, and 18 inches wide. It is covered with Formica and has shelves in it to store books and other items. I keep a small stereo receiver with a set of speakers and a good antenna there to test stereo components. There is

You'll need a test bench to test electronic equipment.

also a cable TV antenna lead and a small 13-inch color TV to test VCRs and televisions. There is a fuse extension outlet with six receptacles for power. I keep blank and prerecorded VHS, VHS-C (compact cassette), and 8mm videotapes and audio cassette tapes and a compact disk under the counter to use when testing any unit. When I sell a piece of electronic equipment, I use this bench to test the item for the customer also. I offer no warranty on electronic equipment except this test to prove that the piece worked when it was sold. Occasionally, there are problems that are not detected on my testing equipment, and I will make accommodations for these.

One thing to watch out for is televisions, VCRs, and stereos that come from rental stores. These rental stores mark their electronic equipment with paint or permanent marker showing the company name and an inventory number. Some people try to erase or cover up these marks and pawn these pieces while they are still under contract. I reject any electronic item that has rental store marks on it if the customer can't prove that it has been paid for.

There are many electronic items you can buy and pawn in your store, including Walkman-type radios, boomboxes, scanners, short-wave radios, mini cassette recorders—the list goes on and on. Just let what your customers pawn and buy help you decide what to risk your money on. Always test items thoroughly, and try to buy them for as little as possible.

Televisions

Televisions (TVs) are fast-selling items in my pawnshop—I never have enough to keep up with the demand. Nearly everyone has at least one TV, and many have more than one, so you will see lots of them brought to your store to be pawned and sold. I pawn and purchase all the televisions I can, although I seldom pawn ones that are more than five years old. I do, however, buy older ones if I don't have any TVs for sale at the time.

Televisions can be checked at your test bench by plugging them in and hooking up an antenna to them. I use cable so I can check all the cable-ready features of the set. If the television came with a remote control when it was new, and almost all current models do, it is worth much less if the remote is missing or broken. Remote controls can be expensive to repair or replace. I once bought a generic brand 20-inch color TV that was missing its remote. I later discovered that the set could not be programmed for cable without the remote, and only a factory remote would work. The manufacturer charged me $48 for a new remote. This, added to the $40 I paid for the set originally, totaled an investment of $88 in a TV worth about $100. It wasn't a loss, but it was too small of a profit. Don't dismiss the possibility that the set has been stolen and the remote left behind.

Once you have the TV plugged in and ready to check, make sure all the buttons on both the TV and the remote work. Find the button that controls the color and turn the color all the way off. Some TVs have one-touch-auto color buttons that can be turned off. Once the color is off, the picture should be totally black and white. If there are lines of color around the subjects in the picture, the set is out of adjustment and needs to be serviced. Next, turn up the brightness to see how much it takes to get a good clear picture. If you turn it up to its maximum level and the picture is still dark, it means that the picture tube is going bad. Be sure to turn up the volume a little to test the sound of the TV. If the sound is garbled and gravelly, the speaker or the speaker output could be blown.

No matter how hard you try, there will always be a TV that gets by you and will have to be repaired.

Unless you can repair them yourself, you will have to find a competent and honest repair person. This can be very difficult, especially finding an honest one, but there are some good TV repair people out there. There is a man down the street from my shop who does all my video repairs, and he is not only competent and honest, but he gives me dealer prices. If you suspect that you are being cheated, there are a few tricks you can use. One is to ask for all the old parts that have been replaced. They can get around this by giving you old parts from other units, but I like to slip in a piece that I know is in perfect working order to see if it gets repaired anyway.

Here are a few guidelines for buying and selling televisions. Orion prints an ***Orion Blue Book for Video and TV***, but I don't use it. I prefer to use local discount stores' catalogs and their sale advertisements to see what new sets are selling for. If a new set sells for $200 in one of these stores, I can usually sell the same set for $150 if it is in like-new condition. As televisions get older, they become worth progressively less. For example, if a one-year-old set is worth $150 retail, then an identical set that is five or six years old may only bring $80. I will pay $40 to $80 for good 20-inch color TVs, $25 to $50 for 13-inch TVs, and $75 to $300 for 25-inch, 27-inch, 31-inch, and larger TVs. I will loan about 10 percent less than these prices. I usually need TVs, so I am often generous.

Videocassette Recorders

Since the early 1980s, VCRs have gained enough popularity that nearly everyone has at least one in their home. When VCRs first appeared, like other new technologies, they were very expensive. Now, they are relatively affordable. To check the correct funtioning of VCRs, you will need an antenna (preferably cable), a color TV, and a VHS videotape. Notice I said VHS and not BETA. Machines that use the BETA system are obsolete and should not be taken. Remote controls are as important for VCRs as they are for TVs. A VCR is marketable without its remote, though it will sell for much less, but some VCRs can't be fully operated without the original factory remote.

To facilitate the testing of VCRs, my cable antenna wire is spliced in the center with quick connectors, so I can leave my test TV hooked up to test the VCR, while the other side has the incoming signal from the cable. I've marked these leads "in from antenna" and "out to TV." In the back of the VCR there is a connection to plug in the cable antenna, which is marked "in." Once you've connected the cable, plug in the power cord and turn the unit on. There is a switch on the VCR in the same area as the cable antenna outlets that lets you select channel three or four. You must set your TV on one of these channels to receive the signal from the VCR. When you turn on the power, most VCRs will automatically take over the channel you have the TV set on. The VCR has a tuner just like a TV, and until you put in a tape to be played, it will show the channel its tuner is set on. Most modern VCRs are cable ready and have auto-program features. Put the unit on "auto program" and let it run through the channels. You will encounter VCRs that have other types of tuner systems, but these will most likely be older models and should be rejected or acquired very cheaply.

When you insert a tape into a VCR, it will automatically bypass its tuner and show what is on the tape. Most VCRs will start playing as soon as you insert the tape, but some will have to be started by pushing the "play" button. It is also good to check the "record" feature by recording off the TV for 30 seconds and then playing the tape back. If you have cable, there is no excuse for recording a poor-quality picture, because the unit records directly from the cable through its own tuner. Check the "rewind" and "fast forward" features of the unit, but make sure it is not in play when you do. I have had machines that would fast forward and rewind while in play, but not do so when the tape was stopped first. These machines had to be repaired.

As I mentioned, Orion publishes an ***Orion Blue Book for Video and TV***, but I don't use it. As with TVs, I prefer to use discount store catalogs to keep up with new retail prices. A good used VCR will sell in my store for about 50 to 60 percent of its new retail price. I will pay $30 to $100 for used VCRs, depending on the brand name and the features they have, and I will sell them for $60 or more. I will loan approximately 10 percent less than the price I will purchase for. The same repairman who fixes my TVs also fixes my VCRs.

Stereo Equipment

Stereo components and speakers are another good source of revenue for any pawnbroker. These items must be checked thoroughly, because any flaw or damage, unless you can repair it yourself, will render the item worthless. Replacement parts can cost even more than the piece is worth. I try to take only newer models with good brand names and reject most of the older silver-colored units.

The ***Orion Blue Book for Audio*** is the bible for buying and selling used stereo equipment. It lists the type of item, year of manufacture, power in watts per channel, model number, new list price, used retail price, and how much to pay for the item depending on its condition, ranging from mint to average. I usually give loans on stereo equipment based on the item being in average condition, which is at the low end of the scale, and I will pay 10 percent more than this to purchase the item. Many people are now buying their stereos as complete systems. These units can be hard to find in the Blue Book, but the discount store catalogs are helpful for making price comparisons.

Receivers

Stereo receivers and amplifier/tuner combinations can be checked on your test bench by hooking them up to some speakers and attaching an FM antenna. When you tune in an FM station, the stereo indicator light should come on. Turn the balance to the left and to the right to make sure that both channels are working. One of the most common problems with stereo receivers is blown output transistors. This problem will be indicated by a weak and gravelly sound coming from one speaker.

Cassette Players

Cassette players can be checked by connecting them to your test receiver. You will need two sets of audio cables with RCA plugs. Your test receiver should have a tape monitor. Play the cassette player through your receiver. You can also record a short section if you wish. Check the "fast forward" and "rewind" functions. Single cassette players have become very difficult to sell because most people want the dual cassette players. My advice is to have a few out for sale and in pawn, but don't let yourself get overstocked.

Equalizers

Equalizers (EQs) can be connected to your receiver through the tape monitor with audio cables, just like a cassette deck. Move the control levers up and down to make sure they work. I can't ever remember getting a bad EQ, so I often don't check them before taking them. EQs are hard to sell, because most of the newer receivers have them built in.

Compact Disk Players

Compact disk players have become very popular. Most people already own a single-play model and want to upgrade to a multi-play model. Consequently, the multi-play models will sell four to one over the single-play models. These units should be tested by using one audio cable to connect it to the CD or auxiliary (AUX) hookup on your receiver. Put in a CD and press "play." If you are using a clean CD and hear the music skip, the unit is either dirty (the lens of the laser diode is dirty), or the unit is broken. CD players are delicate and can break if they are handled roughly.

Speakers

Speakers should be wired into your receiver and listened to carefully. I like to put the volume at a moderate level and put my ear in the center and in front of each speaker in the cabinet. Every speaker should emanate sound. Speaker cabinets with blown speakers in them should be rejected or the price offered for them severely reduced. Damaged grills and scratched veneers will also devalue speakers. The **Orion Blue Book for Audio** is a great resource for pricing speakers.

Complete Stereo Systems

Complete stereo systems are becoming more and more common in the stereo marketplace. Most non-audiophiles find it much simpler to buy a complete matched system rather than mixing and matching stereo components. Complete systems are easier to sell and they make great loan collateral. Don't let the customer bring in just a few pieces at a time and put each piece on a separate pawn ticket. You'll end up investing more money in the system, and you may end up missing some important part. If the unit was meant to be a complete system, have the customer bring in the entire thing. The customer who brings you the system should be able to hook it up and help you check it out. If he has no idea how to operate it, then it may be hot.

Recorded Music and Videotapes

Recorded music, as long as it is in the form of a compact disk, can be a good money-maker. Cassette tapes and albums are a dead market. I take CDs for purchase only, and I pay $1.50 each for them and sell them for $5 each or 5 for $20. I also buy videotaped movies once in a while, mostly for my own collection. Most of them can be purchased for $2 or $3.

Video Game Systems

Many pawnbrokers take video game systems in pawn, but I pass on most of them. There is some demand for them during Christmastime, but I've seen these things become obsolete overnight. Whenever some hotshot computer genius creates a new and improved model, I get stuck with a bunch of plastic junk that nobody wants to buy. If you want to take these items, my advice is to purchase them only, don't take them in pawn, and buy only the newest models. Never pay more than 10 or 20 cents on the dollar of their new retail price.

HOUSEHOLD ITEMS

Many pawnbrokers take antiques, oriental rugs, clocks, and other furniture in pawn. If you have the space and are knowledgeable about this type of merchandise, it can be profitable to pawn and purchase these items. I have taken old clocks, fine crystal, porcelain figurines, and some furniture, but I have only limited knowledge about these items. I usually rely on my trusty discount store catalogs or an Army Air Force Exchange Service (AAFES) catalog that a friend got for me to see what these or similar items cost new. There are also many price guides available at your local bookstore that cover all these items. A general rule of thumb is to buy household items at prices a little higher than what you could sell them to other dealers for. This way, if you are unable to sell them in your store at retail, you can take them to an auction or wholesale them to another dealer and still make money. My house is full of items like Baccarat crystal, Lladro figurines, and antique clocks, which I pawned or purchased for 10 percent of their original retail price.

MUSICAL INSTRUMENTS AND ACCESSORIES

Musical instruments and related merchandise have been a real money-making part of my business for many years. At the end of every school year, students want to sell their band instruments, and at the beginning of the new school year, these instruments are in high demand again. I am usually able to sell all the used band instruments I can get. Instruments that are especially popular are trumpets, saxophones, trombones, and flutes. In fact, President Bill Clinton stimulates the popularity of saxophones with each appearance he makes playing his.

There are plenty of collectors, part-time musicians, and professional musicians who are looking for a deal on higher quality musical instruments. Every Christmas, I am able to sell all the inexpensive electric guitars, acoustic guitars, and amplifiers I get. I also sell new items like strings, picks, straps, mouthpieces, harmonicas, cases, and other accessories. There are always lots of musicians who want to pawn their "axes" so they can pay their rent or utility bill.

Orion prints a Blue Book for musical instruments, vintage guitars, and professional sound equipment. Blue Book Publications (see Appendix E) has also come out with a book of guitar values. I have not seen it yet, but if it is as good as their book on guns, it should be useful. When I use the Orion books, I tend to follow their guidelines for prices to purchase used musical instruments, and I will loan about 10 percent less than that.

Brass Instruments

Brass instruments include trumpets, French horns, trombones, baritones, and tubas. Brass instruments are easily dented, and while small nicks and dents are to be expected on used instruments, large dents are unacceptable. All valves and slides should be well oiled or greased and should not bind or stick. The instrument should have a case and a mouthpiece. Most horns come with either a brass or a silver finish. Some wear and discoloration is acceptable but will make these instruments worth slightly less.

Percussion Instruments

Percussion instruments are those played by being struck with mallets, sticks, or the hands. This includes drums of all types, cymbals, bells, and xylophones. Drums should have all their bracing hardware and good heads without holes. Heads can be replaced easily, but the heads themselves can be expensive. In fact, drum parts in general can be easy to replace, but you should take the cost of the parts into account when you offer a price. If a drum is meant to have legs or stands, these should be included. Drums without their stands are like TVs without their remotes: hard to sell. Cymbals with cracks in them aren't good for anything but scrap brass.

Woodwind Instruments

Woodwind instruments include clarinets, saxophones, oboes, piccolos, and flutes. These instruments must be inspected closely for damage to their corks and pads, because these parts wear out regularly and have to be replaced. To repad, recork, and adjust one of these instruments can cost $75 to $250 or more. For example, I sell average student-grade clarinets for about $150. If I didn't know the instrument needed new pads and corks and paid $50 dollars for it, I would be lucky to make any profit at all after I spent $75 or more to have it repaired. Instruments in need of any repairs should be purchased for well below the price listed under the "average condition" column in the ***Orion Blue Book for Guitars and Musical Instruments*** or rejected entirely if the piece is too far gone. To completely overhaul a musical instrument can cost $110 to $600 or more. I not only inspect an instrument myself but also have the customer put it together and play it. This the best way to see if the instrument is in playing condition. If the customer claims to own it, then he should be able to play it. If he can't play it, it doesn't necessarily mean the piece is stolen, but he'd better have a good explanation.

Keyboards and Electronic Pianos

While I won't take large wooden upright or grand pianos, portable keyboards and electronic pianos are very profitable. There are two types of electronic pianos: the small-key type and standard-key type. The small-key variety is just a toy for entertainment, and I don't often deal with those. The standard-key variety, which has the same size keys as large pianos, is what most people are looking for. Today's modern electronic keyboards are like complete orchestras. They can duplicate any instrument, they have sound effects, and they can even applaud themselves. Many are MIDI-adaptable, which means they can work through a computer.

To check the proper functioning of a keyboard, plug in the adapter or put in some fresh batteries and play it. Electric pianos, while similar to electronic keyboards, are hooked up slightly differently. They usually run directly off 110-volt power and require an amplifier, which should be made to handle a bass guitar or keyboard. I like to check every key all the way up the scale and all the features, and I have the owner demonstrate the features for me. If it belongs to them, they should be able to demonstrate its features.

The ***Orion Blue Book for Guitars and Musical Instruments*** covers all brands of keyboards, and when I use it, I purchase at the average price and loan about 10 percent less than that. One thing to remember is that the new retail list price quoted in the Blue Book is the manufacturer's suggested price. The local Kmart sells keyboards for far less than this price. Sometimes you must pay a little less than the book suggests to be able to sell your used merchandise at a price that can compete. This can be true for anything listed in these Blue Books.

Stringed Instruments

Stringed instruments include violins, violas, cellos, basses, banjos, mandolins, guitars, and any other instrument with strings. The ***Orion Blue Book for Guitars and Musical Instruments*** is useful to price these items, but sometimes it is hard to tell what model some instruments are. They aren't always marked with a model name or number. You should order some wholesale and retail catalogs so you can compare prices. If you can't figure out what model an instrument is, you can at least compare it to a similar model that is currently available. If I can buy a new instrument that is similar to a used instrument for $100 wholesale, then I expect to purchase the used one for $50 and loan about 10 percent less than that. Again, have the customer tune and play his stringed instrument, if possible, even if you have to suffer through a little bad music. Make sure everything needed to play the instrument is present.

Orchestra Instruments

The model names or numbers of orchestra instruments, such as violins, are especially hard to determine. Since most of the instruments I see are student grade, I will price any unknown models in that category. Violins and similar instruments need to come with at least one bow that is in good condition. Many customers have come into my store with violins marked with the Stradivarius name thinking they had an original that was built by the 17th-century master, only to have their bubble burst when I point out the small print on the label that says "Made in West Germany." Never bet the farm on any instrument someone says is valuable. If you are offered an extremely valuable piece, get an expert's opinion before you make any large investments. We've all heard the tale about the guy who buys an old violin at a flea market for 10 bucks and later finds out it's worth $10 million. This could happen to you, but the odds are about the same as winning the lottery.

Guitars and Accessories

Of all instruments, guitars are pawned and sold most often, and you may come across some valuable collector's models. But keep in mind that collectible guitars can vary in price with changing fads. If, for example, some rock star shows up on TV with a vintage model guitar, its market value can go way up. But the next week, the same guitar can be worth half as much, because another rock star played a different model on TV, and everyone suddenly wants one like his.

There are two basic categories of guitars: acoustic and electric. Acoustic guitars are hollow sound boxes with fretted necks that make their sounds acoustically, while electric guitars make their sounds through electronic pickups and amplifiers. The two kinds of electric guitars are lead guitars, which have six strings, and bass guitars, which normally have four strings. Acoustic guitars can have six or twelve strings.

On acoustic guitars, make sure the neck is straight and not bowed, and look for stress cracks between the neck and body of the guitar. On electric guitars, check the pickups to make sure they work. Electric guitar amplifiers are sometimes pawned as well. I recommend that you have at least one lead guitar amplifier and one bass amplifier on hand to check electric guitars as they come in. All the tuning heads and other hardware on both types of guitars should be present and work properly. Broken, cracked, dirty, and abused guitars are virtually worthless. Cases are a definite plus, and I will sometimes reject guitars that don't have them.

The Blue Book lists these items, and I always try to buy them for the price listed at the low end of the "average condition" category and loan around 10 percent less than that.

OFFICE EQUIPMENT

Of all office equipment, you will deal with computers foremost. I prefer to take mostly IBM and IBM clones with 386, 486, or Pentium processors. I am not that knowledgeable about Macintosh or Apple computers, but I have taken some of the higher-end models. You can also take typewriters, word processors, adding machines, safes, copiers, fax machines, telephones, and other equipment.

The best way to test these items is to have the customer set them up and make them work. Make sure you get the complete system before you hand over any money. For example, computers should have monitors, copiers should have cartridges, and so on.

I find the best way to price these items is by comparing them with similar merchandise in discount store and office supply store catalogs. I can sell office equipment for 50 or 60 percent of its new retail price, so I will buy items for 25 or 30 percent of their new retail price and loan about 10 percent less than that.

OPTICAL EQUIPMENT

Binoculars, microscopes, telescopes, transits, sextants, rifle scopes, and many other optical instruments have been pawned in my pawnshop. Binoculars are especially popular. I see a lot of cheap optical equipment that is sold in the discount stores, but I do get some of the better quality equipment also. The cheap stuff can sell for about half of what the discount stores sell it for, which is pretty cheap. I have seen binoculars sold at Kmart for as little as $20. If you sell them for $10, then you shouldn't pay more than $5 for them.

High quality used optics are much harder to find and consequently will sell for 50 or 60 percent of their new retail price. Purchase them for 25 to 30 percent of their new retail price and loan about 10 percent less than that. Wholesale gun distributors' catalogs are good sources for pricing binoculars, telescopes, and rifle scopes. Other optics are harder to reference. For some items, I've had to look up dealers in the yellow pages and ask for prices. I just give them a general description of the item as though I'm shopping for one.

Optical equipment is very delicate and should be

checked over thoroughly. Glass lenses can crack or shatter, prisms can be jarred out of alignment, and the inert gases inside can leak out. Check binoculars by looking through them at a perpendicular object, like a tree or a telephone pole in the distance. If there appears to be two objects or when you close one eye at a time the object changes position, the prisms are out of alignment. Unless the binoculars are of high quality, reject them. They can be repaired, but it will cost at least $60. I once bought a pair of Nazi-issue World War II binoculars for $20 that I knew were in need of repair. It cost me $60 to get them fixed, and I sold them for $150.

PHOTOGRAPHIC EQUIPMENT

This category includes cameras, lenses, video cameras, and related equipment. Thirty-five millimeter cameras and video camcorders are highest in demand. Notice that I said video camcorders and not video cameras. Video camcorders are video cameras that have internal videotape recording, and you should only deal with these. There are still many of the older video cameras around that need separate recording packs, and you may see some of the professional nonrecording video cameras. Avoid all of these units. Most people who come to your store looking for a video camera just want an ordinary camcorder to take family pictures, and anything else will be hard to sell. You will see 35mm cameras more than any other photographic equipment. The best brands are Minolta, Canon, Nikon, Pentax, and Olympus. There are other brands, but these are the main ones I deal with.

There are two guide books that can help you price photographic items. One is the ***Camera Price Data***

Book by the Charlotte Camera Group, and the other is the ***Orion Blue Book for Cameras*** (see Appendix E). When buying photographic equipment, stay on the low side of the price recommendations, and pay 10 percent less than that for loans. You can also use discount store catalog prices as a guide and buy things at 25 percent less than retail and loan 10 percent less than that. This works especially well for the small automatic 35mm cameras that have become so popular.

When video camcorders and 35mm cameras are brought in for purchase or for a loan, I ask the owners to demonstrate how the item works and show me its features. If they can't find the shutter, open the back to load film, change a lens, or load a videotape, then the item may not belong to them. When I check a video camcorder, I record some test film of the person who brought it in. I then rewind the tape and play it back through the monitor on the camera to make sure it is working properly. I won't tape over this portion of film for two weeks or more so the tape can be used as evidence if the camera turns out to be stolen.

To check 35mm single-lens reflex (SLR) cameras, open the back and look through the lens while setting the shutter at different speeds to make sure the camera is working. Also, look through the viewfinder and make sure the light meter is working. Many newer automatic cameras set all the functions of the camera themselves. By aiming the camera toward a light and then toward a darker area, you should be able to see the meter change or see the camera automatically adjust itself. The most popular cameras on today's market are the autofocus 35mm SLR models. These cameras offer the changeable lens of the SLR and also focus automatically. Check this autofocus feature by aiming the camera at objects at different ranges, making sure it focuses properly.

There are also less expensive range-finder autofocus automatic cameras. These are not as easy to check as the others, but they don't cost as much either. Most of them won't be listed in the camera price guides, so I usually rely on the discount catalogs. For most of these cameras, I won't usually pay more than $20 to purchase them. The only way to check them is to turn them on, push the shutter button, and see if they focus, take a picture, and wind the film to the next frame. Most of these cameras have built-in flashes that should also be checked.

I have found that most cameras that are clean and well cared for work properly. Always avoid cameras that are dirty, beat up, and scratched. I have seen old Nikons that look like they have been through the war, and even though they work, they are nearly unsalable. Dirt, beach sand, and moisture can quickly ruin a delicate camera. Any moisture at all can ruin the electronics in the more modern cameras. Since most camera repair shops won't even open the case of a camera before they give a repair estimate for less than $50, the cost to repair any camera can quickly exceed its value.

Many photographic accessories will come into your store to be sold or pawned as well, such as lenses, flashes, winders, filters, dark room equipment, tripods, and other items, and the appraisal books will list most of them. You will also see a lot of the older obsolete cameras, and because cameras suffer from the same planned obsolescence that other electronic equipment does, there is a limited market for them. Don't let yourself get overstocked with old cameras. Some camera buyers are listed in Appendix E of this book that will buy your excess inventory, but they're only interested in certain models, and they want them cheap.

SILVERWARE

Silver flatware and hollowware are always in demand. They must, of course, be solid silver, because silver-plated items aren't worth much. I always value silverware by the actual silver content in the piece. I will weigh it on my scale and estimate how much pure silver is in it. If I'm weighing a set of flatware, I will take each piece from a setting and weigh it, then multiply their weights by the number of settings there are. Large pieces of hollowware are sometimes too big to fit on my scale, so I must guess at the weight. Once I figure out the weight in troy ounces, I multiply this by the current spot price per ounce for pure silver. I also take into account that silverware is only 92.5 percent pure silver, which means I must adjust the spot price of silver by 92.5 percent. For example, if the spot price for silver is $4 per ounce, silverware is worth $3.70 per ounce. I would purchase it for $3 per ounce (about 80 percent of spot price) and loan $2.50 per ounce (about 70 percent of spot price).

Atlantic Silver Incorporated (see Appendix E) offers a free pattern identification booklet. Rare patterns can sell for a premium, and even common patterns will sell for at least twice their silver value. Engraved initials will devalue silverware unless it belonged to a famous individual. The booklet also has pictures of trademarks and proof marks that can help you determine if a piece is solid silver. The main marks to look for that indicate if a piece is solid silver and not silver plate is the word "sterling" or the numbers 925 (92.5 percent).

SPORTING GOODS

This category includes a lot of merchandise. Most of it can be priced in discount department store catalogs, and many items can also be looked up in one of the wholesale archery, gun, or knife catalogs listed in Appendix E. Some of the best sporting good items to take are camping gear, compound bows and archery equipment, fishing gear, golf clubs, exercise equipment, and knives.

Knives have been good selling items in my shop, and I buy and pawn all the good ones I can. I also stock a large selection of new knives. Compound bows sell well just before hunting season, but I have to be careful not to get overstocked, because they are hard to sell the rest of the year. They must also be checked over carefully to make sure that they have not be abused and are not in need of repair. I buy bows for about 40 percent of their wholesale price, and I will pawn them for about 30 percent of their wholesale price. You must be able to sell bows and many other sporting goods below wholesale to compete with the discount stores.

There are a lot of sporting goods that I won't normally take, some of which are bowling balls, tennis rackets, snow and water skis, and roller skates. It's up to you to take what you want in your shop, but I have found that these items are hard to sell.

TEMPERATURE CONTROL APPLIANCES

This category includes fans, air conditioners, heaters,

humidifiers, and dehumidifiers. These appliances can be profitable, but you must be careful not to take bad ones. The cost of even a small repair can wipe out all your profit. My father deals with these items more than I, and he takes in all the air conditioners he can during the winter months and is able to sell them all before the end of summer. He does the same with small electric and kerosene heaters during the summer months.

Air conditioners should be checked on your test bench by plugging them in and running them for five or ten minutes. They should be blowing cold air by then. I won't take the the big 220-volt units because they're too big to handle, and I don't have an outlet to plug them into. Electric heaters should be plugged in and run also. Kerosene heaters don't need to be lit, but they should have plenty of wick left.

Most of these items are listed in department store catalogs, and you can sell used ones for 50 to 60 percent of their new retail cost. You should loan about 25 percent their retail cost and purchase them for 30 percent of their retail cost. During a heat wave, I have seen Kmart and Wal-Mart run out of portable air conditioners and other dealers start gouging prices on these units. I don't do this. People will remember if I treat them fairly, and they will become repeat customers.

TOOLS

Buying and pawning used tools is a very profitable part of the pawnshop business. It seems that everyone always needs more tools. There are people who come by my shop once or twice a week to make sure they don't miss a chance to buy any new items I might put out in my used tool section. Some of them get so excited you would think they just hit the jackpot on a one-armed bandit. One of my customers would break out in a sweat and start trembling when he came in and saw freshly stocked sets of Mac and Snap-on tools. The first time it happened, I thought I might have to call 911. But most people just want a good deal and will be much calmer.

I put most of my Snap-on, Mac, and Craftsman tools in this show-case, because they are easy to slip into a pocket.

Hand Tools

There are three big names in the hand tool business: Craftsman, Mac, and Snap-on. Snap-on tools are the best and most expensive, while Mac and Craftsman are close seconds, but Mac tools are slightly more costly than Craftsman. You should keep a current catalog on hand for each of these companies. The Craftsman tool catalog can be obtained easily from Sears, but the other two are more difficult to get. Snap-on and Mac tools are sold only by dealers off of their trucks. These dealers go to shops where professional mechanics work and sell directly to them.

There are a few other good brands of tools, but just about any tool that says it's made in America will make good collateral and be easy to sell. What are less desirable are the Chinese, Taiwanese, and Korean-made tools. These will sell, but they are hardly worth the time it takes to put price tags on them. I sell large Ziplock bags of 100 Taiwan sockets for $5 per bag and Chinese wrenches for 50 cents per wrench.

Craftsman, Mac, and Snap-on tools will easily sell for at least half of their retail price. Some hand tools like wrenches and sockets, if they are in sets and in like-new condition, will sell for up to 70 percent of their listed price. Sets of tools made by the big three brand names should be purchased for 25 or 30 percent of their retail price. Loan at least 25 percent of that and hope the customer doesn't come back for them. Other brands of American tools should be purchased for about 50 percent less than a similar Craftsman tool. For example, I will pay 10 to 25 cents apiece for sockets, 25 cents apiece for small wrenches, 50 cents apiece for medium-sized wrenches, $1 or more apiece for large wrenches, and $1 to $5 each for adjustable wrenches, pliers, vise grips, or snips. These tools should sell for at least twice what you pay for them.

When people bring in boxes of tools, they usually have a mix of quality and cheap tools. I will carefully inventory a box of tools to see if there are any

People love to dig into my tools.

sets, and I always offer a little more if the box and any other marketable items are included. I have found all sorts of things in people's tool boxes, including drugs. (This is something to look out for in anything you take. It might be hard to explain to a detective who comes in to check for stolen property and finds drugs in your business how the drugs got there. Anytime you find drugs in an item to be pawned, have the customer get them out of your store immediately or flush them yourself. Don't take any chances.) The average box of tools that comes into my store can be pawned or purchased for $40 to $50. You can sell this box of tools broken down into sets and individual pieces for a total of $100 to $125. I always break up a box of tools into separate pieces and sets because I can make a much better profit this way. It's a little more work, but it's worth it.

Most people who come in to buy tools are looking for pieces to improve the sets they already have. I put all my loose tools in tubs on a counter for people to dig through. Loose sockets are put in separate tubs, and their prices are posted on the wall behind them. Any miscellaneous leftover junk that I find in a toolbox is dumped into a bargain box labeled 50 cents apiece.

Power Tools

Power tools are also brought in regularly for loans and purchases. Mac, Snap-on, and Craftsman are also the best brands in power tools. There are both electric and pneumatic tools. Pneumatic tools can't be checked unless you have an air compressor. If you take them and you don't have a compressor to test them, you must get them cheaply. Air tools are also hard to sell if you don't have a compressor to demonstrate that they work properly. I buy and pawn air-powered mechanic's and carpenter's tools for about 10 cents on the dollar of their retail value, unless the customer has a compressor with him to demonstrate how well they work. While the three big tool companies give lifetime warranties on their hand tools, they won't give them on their pneumatic tools. Parts kits are available to rebuild these tools, but it is a pain in the butt. It is best to buy these tools cheap, sell them cheap, not worry, and be happy.

Electric tools are easy to check for proper functioning. Just plug them in at your test bench and let them run. You can even keep some scrap wood around to cut with the saws or drill with the drills. Electric tools should have good cords, and there shouldn't be sparks flying or a burning plastic smell when they are running. Avoid tools that have been abused, as they will be hard to sell. Construction workers are especially bad about abusing their tools and will try to sell you worn-out junk.

I keep tool catalogs from several discount stores and warehouse stores in addition to the Craftsman catalog to find out what these tools sell for new. Most any electric power tool will sell for at least half of what it cost new. You should purchase these tools for 25 percent of their retail price and loan about 20 percent.

YARD EQUIPMENT

Lawnmowers, tillers, weed trimmers, blowers, garden tools, chain saws, chippers/shredders, log splitters, and other types of yard equipment are also pawned or sold. Lawn equipment sells best in the spring and summer, but chain saws and log splitters will sell whenever you get them. The catalogs for the discount tool centers will help you price most of these items. Sears also has a specialty catalog for these items. Most will sell for half of their new retail price. You should purchase them for 25 percent of their retail price and pawn them for 20 percent. I like to have the customer take the gas-powered tools in front of the shop and start them up. I keep mixed and unmixed fuel on hand if the tanks are empty. Electric tools should be tested on your bench. Avoid taking equipment that is broken, abused, or hard to start.

8 Merchandising, Advertising, and Bookkeeping

If you've read this far, you now know the history of pawnbroking, where to put your new pawnshop, how to keep it secure, how to be a pawnbroker and how to buy, sell, and pawn merchandise. There are three more subjects you need to know to keep your business running smoothly. They are merchandising, advertising, and bookkeeping. In this chapter, I offer suggestions on stocking your showroom and buying new merchandise to stock it; discuss yellow page ads, road signs, and other advertising; and make a few suggestions on handling all the money you'll be raking in.

MERCHANDISING

Before opening my pawnshop for the first day of regular business, I had managed to acquire a modest inventory of goods to sell. Much of my inventory had been purchased from my father's pawnshop over the previous six-month period. I also bought some new items, like inexpensive handguns and knives. Some of the used items I had were jewelry, hand tools, power tools, a couple of small TVs, and a VCR. Many of these items came from my home, and I also had a personal collection of firearms, knives, and ammunition that I added to my shop inventory. Even with all this, my shelves looked pitifully empty. I remember buying a sign-making kit and putting little signs in my showcases and on my shelves. They said "cameras," "jewelry," "guns," "knives," "tools," and "coins" so people would know what I planned to fill all the empty spaces with. It wasn't long before I had to remove these signs so they didn't block the view of items they referred to.

When you first open your store, you may wonder if the empty spaces will ever be filled, but before long, you may not have enough room. One good source for

When a customer enters my shop, he sees well-stocked shelves and gets a good impression.

used merchandise is your own home. Take a good look at everything you own, and see if there aren't some things you could live without for awhile. Anything you are able to give up can be replaced later on with items you get in your shop, and you can probably replace them with something newer and better. I find that I am always replacing something at home when a better item comes into my pawnshop. I just put the old item out for sale. I replace at least one TV and one VCR every year. I think of most of the things in my home as floating inventory for my shop, and I account for the cost price of these items in my yearly tax inventory. This way, I don't have to pay state sales tax on the items I take home, because although I'm using them, they are still part of my shop inventory until I sell them. It's like I'm getting them for free, because I will eventually sell them and make a profit. I sometimes get permission from my customers to use their things while they are in pawn. As long as I don't break or abuse their things, they usually don't mind, and I often give them a break on their interest. This enables me to sell things that I use or may need, because I have use of the same items as long as they are in pawn.

Garage sales and flea markets are also good sources for inventory to stock a new pawnshop. Just make sure you buy things at prices that will allow you to make a 20 to 50 percent markup so you can make a profit. I have several customers who go to garage sales every Saturday and bring me some of their finds. They will often sell the items to me and make a profit, then I will resell the same items and also make a profit.

Buying new merchandise is the easiest way to stock your new store. I recommend that you spend at least $5,000 on new inventory. That may seem like a lot, but it's not. You'll still have plenty of empty space to fill. Many wholesalers are listed in the appendices. Before you order from any of them, get their catalogs and comparison shop. There can be a 10 to 30 percent difference in price for the same items from different companies.

Once you've made the decision to become a pawnbroker, start accumulating inventory six months to a year before you plan to open for business. Don't be ashamed to ask for donations from friends and relatives. Clean out grandma's attic or garage, and offer people credit that can be used in your shop after you've gotten going. Once you've opened for business, your customers can be your best source of merchandise to sell. Many people who come to make a loan will often sell if you ask them and offer them a little more money.

The following is a list of new merchandise that, in my opinion, should be carried by every pawnbroker.

Firearms

- Two .380-caliber semiauto pistols. I like the Bryco/Jennings models. Get two different styles with different finishes.
- One .22-caliber and one .25-caliber semiauto pistol. Bryco/Jennings models are good.
- Two 9mm semiauto pistols. Get different models. I like the Interarms Helwan and the Jennings Model 59.
- Two .38-caliber revolvers. Get one Charco/ Charter Arms and one Rossi 2-inch snub-nosed in blue or stainless steel.

You can buy more and better quality handguns, and you can also buy some inexpensive long guns. The eight handguns listed here will cost at least $800. If the gun business looks promising in your area, you can stock holsters, cleaning kits, spare magazines, and other accessories. I recommend you order a dealer's pack of handgun pouches and inexpensive long gun cases from Ace Case Company or Brauer Brothers (see Appendix D). Most of these cases cost less than $2, and you can make a 100-percent markup on them. They also come in handy to cinch that tough gun sale.

If you are in an area where it is tough to sell handguns, there are other alternatives. Pistol-grip and other defensive-type shotguns can be good sellers. Military surplus rifles are quite popular, especially U.S. guns like M1 Garands and .30-caliber carbines. There are also self-defense products like Mace, pepper spray, stun guns, and personal alarms.

When I first opened, I did a lot of special orders for customers who wanted the more expensive firearms. I would order any gun and charge the customer 10 percent more than wholesale, but my minimum fee was $25. The customer also had to pay for the gun in advance plus the shipping, handling, COD fees, and taxes.

Ammunition

- Ten boxes each of .38 special round-nosed lead (RNL) reloads, .380 auto full metal jacket (FMJ), and 9mm parabellum FMJ
- Five boxes each of .45 auto FMJ, .25 auto FMJ, .44 magnum jacketed hollowpoint (JHP), and .32 auto FMJ
- Three bricks (30 boxes) of .22-caliber long rifle ammo. (Buy this on sale at your local Kmart or Wal-Mart store.)
- Five boxes each of 7.62 x 39 softpoint (SP), .223

FMJ, .30-30 SP, .308 SP, .243 SP, and .30-06 SP
· Five boxes of 12-gauge 00 buckshot

If you shop the catalogs and buy reloads or generic brands, this ammo should cost around $650. You should have ammo in these basic calibers in stock to sell and to be able to test-fire guns when necessary. Sometimes I will include a box of ammo with a gun to make the sale or offer ammo instead of discounting the price of a gun.

Knives
As far as I am concerned, there is only one place to buy knives, and that is Blue Ridge Knives in Marion, Virginia. By all means shop around, but get a catalog before you order. You should make an initial investment of around $500 in knives. Reproduction swords and surplus bayonets are real eye catchers in a showcase. I like commemorative and collector's editions also. Work and hunting knives are good sellers, as are self-defense-type blades such as butterflies and boot knives. Avoid the cheap flea market junk made in Pakistan and China. I have three showcases full of knives, 80 percent of which are new.

Musical Instruments
· Two 1/2-size acoustic guitars
· Two 3/4-size acoustic guitars
· Two full-size acoustic guitars. Buy the package deal if you can, which includes the case and strap. Get different models.
· One electric lead guitar. Get an inexpensive model and a package deal, if available.
· One electric bass guitar. Get an inexpensive model

My musical instrument department is well-stocked and set up to catch the eye.

and a package deal, if available.
- One electric lead guitar amplifier. Get an inexpensive model.
- One electric bass guitar amplifier. Get an inexpensive model.
- Twelve 10-foot long metal-end guitar cables
- Twelve 20-foot long metal-end guitar cables
- Two inexpensive guitar cables
- Twenty-four Peg-Board guitar hangers (for your display)
- Four inexpensive guitar stands
- Twelve packs of electric guitar strings
- Twelve packs of acoustic guitar strings
- Twelve packs of ball-end nylon classical acoustic guitar strings
- Six packs of bass guitar strings. Buy promotional

or generic strings.
· One guitar pick assortment
· Twelve basic guitar straps

These items should cost about $800. You can also stock harmonicas, bongo drums, drum sets, and other new instruments, microphones, mike stands, mouthpieces, cases, parts, and other accessories. I recommend that you keep your initial investment down to around $1,000 until demand warrants a larger inventory. If you get a good deal of interest and special requests from your customers, you can stock everything a regular music store does. You can also do special orders for things you don't have in stock.

Jewelry

Several jewelry wholesalers are listed in Appendix C. Order eight or ten different catalogs and do some comparison shopping. Think about spending $1,000 to $1,500 on new jewelry. I recommend that you not buy any diamond jewelry, and limit the amount of colored stone jewelry you buy. You'll get more for your money if you buy chains, bracelets, earrings, charms, and rings without stones.

There are a lot of 10k gold pieces available now, but I prefer the 14k pieces, even though they are slightly more expensive. Don't buy 16-inch chains, because 18-inch, 20-inch, and longer chains sell much better. Rope and link chains are better to buy than some of the herringbone chains, which tend to kink badly.

When you buy new jewelry to sell retail, you will be in competition with the discount stores. Don't expect to make more than about a 50-percent markup on these items.

Other Merchandise

If you have any money left over, get a copy of *Close Out News* and order some catalogs from general merchandise and electronics wholesalers (see Appendix E). You can buy new tools, electronics, and anything else that you think might sell to stock your pawnshop.

ADVERTISING

The advertising lifeline for any pawnbroker is his Yellow Pages listing. At least 95 percent of all new customers who call my shop found my phone number in the Yellow Pages. I even timed the opening of my pawnshop to coincide with the distribution of the new phone book. I rented my shop space three months in advance just so I could have an address and phone number to list. This worked out well, because I had plenty of time to set up shop, install security devices, and start acquiring the things I needed to open for business. I chose the name Alexander's American Pawn Company so my ad would be at the top of the listings for pawnshops in the yellow pages. Since I couldn't afford a large ad until my shop became more established, this enabled me to use an in-column ad and still get a lot of attention on a page full of other pawnshop ads.

You must decide what you want to spend on advertising. A half-page ad in a medium-sized city's phone directory can cost more than a month's rent. I recommend that you start off modestly and increase your ad size every year. I have been in business for more than 10 years, and I am now up to a quarter-page ad, which costs $500 per month. Added to this are my other ads, services, and my phone bill, which comes to more than $600

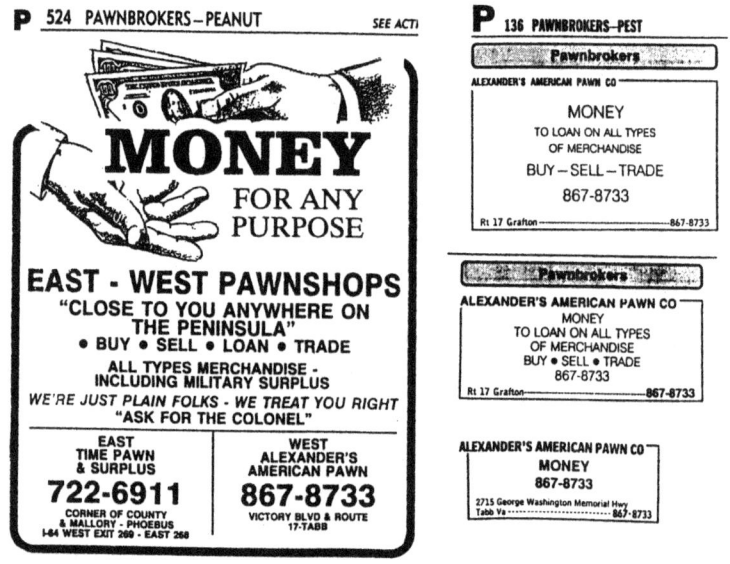

Yellow Pages advertising is a pawnbroker's lifeline.

per month. That's what my monthly rent was when I first opened my pawnshop.

Road signs can also be an effective means to advertise your pawnshop. When I first opened, county ordinances prevented me from constructing as large a sign as I wanted. I had to settle for a smaller sign, but I emphasized three words on it: Pawnshop, Guns, and Gold. I also had the three-golden-balls pawnshop symbol on each side of the front of my building. The three golden balls are universally recognized as the symbol for pawnshops. As such, they provide a big advantage to pawnbrokers over most other merchants, because anytime the symbol is displayed on a business, it is instantly recognized as a pawnshop.

A road sign, although an expensive initial invest-

Your storefront should be clean and inviting. Red, black, and yellow are highly visible colors for signs.

Unique objects like this cannon can attract people's attention when they pass by.

ment, is one of the cheapest ways to advertise your business. A well-made electric sign will promote your pawnshop 24 hours a day, seven days a week, 365 days a year. Another way to advertise to road traffic is to use any glass windows you may have as signs. A lettering kit can be used to say anything you want.

There are many other forms of advertising you can use to promote your business. I tried radio, TV, direct mail, handbills, newspaper ads, and promotional items like pens, key chains, and matchbooks and found that the effects of most of these were marginal at best. The television ads I tried were aired on a local cable access channel, and I was not impressed with the results. The regional newspaper is so expensive to advertise in that they have nearly priced me out of the market. They even charge triple the normal rates to dealers for their classified ads. There is a small weekly county and community newspaper in my area, and their rates are much more reasonable. It is my opinion that the best advertising value for this type of business is the Yellow Pages.

BOOKKEEPING

Managing the cash flow of a pawnshop business is very important. You must keep accurate books or risk trouble with the tax man. In 10 years of doing business, I have never had any problems with the Internal Revenue Service (IRS) or the Virginia Department of Taxation. Part of this success can be attributed to the way I think of my business. I consider my business to be a separate entity. If you become incorporated, you must also think of your business as separate entity, just as if it were a person. If you think of your business as a separate person, you will be more careful about keeping good records on how much you put into it and how much you take out of it. I am still a sole proprietor, but the day is rapidly approaching when I will form a corporation. The only real reason to do this is to protect my personal assets from any lawsuits arising from problems that may occur during the conduct of my business. If you have substantial personal assets, it may be in your best interest to incorporate.

As a self-employed individual, you will need to keep records on several business activities to be able to do your yearly taxes. These are your inventory at the beginning and end of the year, your total sales, the cost of the goods sold, the income from the interest on loans made, and expenses incurred from doing business. The last one is probably the most important, but you must keep accurate records for all of them for proof.

At the beginning and end of each year, you must add up the actual cost of each item that is for sale in your store. The cost of items that are in pawn should not be included in this total. The number of sales you make should be taken from sales tax returns that you send in each month. The amount you report to the state and the IRS should match exactly. The cost of goods sold should be taken from the pawn tickets of forfeited pledges and amount of the items sold that you purchased from customers and wholesalers. The figure for the amount of interest received from loans can be taken from your register balance sheets, which are discussed in the next section.

The last item is the one that gets most people in trouble, and that's business expenses. This is where treating your business like a separate entity really pays off. Every time you pay a bill with a check or buy supplies with cash, there should be a receipt to prove where the money went. It's like your boss gave you money to buy something, and he wants a receipt and the change. Your business expenses will include items like advertising, phone bills, electric bills, rent, wages for employees (this is a separate tax nightmare), office supplies, and repairs. You must have a receipt as proof of each expense incurred.

Balancing the Cash Register
When I first opened for business, I couldn't afford a real cash register. I got by with a cash drawer that was mounted under the counter where the cashier's window

was. I kept track of all transactions, including sales and interest, by writing receipts and jamming them on a spindle made for that purpose. I still use that old spindle today to keep any receipts I need, but I now have a cash register to add up all my transactions. A cash register is really just an adding machine that keeps a running total of how much money is put into it or taken out of it. All the transactions done on my register are categorized into departments. I have eight departments programmed into my register, which are separated into incoming and outgoing departments. Money coming into the business should be put into the taxable sales, nontaxable sales, payment of principle, payment of interest, or payment of layaway departments. Money going out should be put into the loan, purchase, or other expenses departments. The following is the sheet I use to balance my register.

Date _____

Sales Recapitulation

Taxable sales	_____
Sales tax	_____
Nontaxable sales	_____
Total	_____
Less: Layaways	_____
Plus: Payments on layaways	_____
Loan principal	_____
Loan interest	_____
Subtotal	_____
Plus: Additional operating cash	_____
Total	_____

Cash Proof

Total money in drawer   _____
Less: Starting operational cash   _____
Subtotal (cash on hand)   _____
Plus: Cash paid out as loans   _____
      as purchases   _____
Plus refunds: Merchandise   _____
      Sales tax   _____
Plus: Other expenses   _____
Total   _____

Operational Cash

Starting operational cash   _____
Plus: Additional from cash on hand   _____
or,
Less: Reduction to operational cash by deposit _____
Total: Ending operational cash   _____

Deposit

Cash on hand (from line three in Cash Proof)   _____
Less: Additional operational cash   _____
or,
Plus: Reduction to operational cash by deposit _____
Total available for deposit   _____

If you have employees, it is wise to balance your register every day. I used to balance mine once a week before I started hiring employees. By balancing your register daily, you will be able to correct any mistakes easily. You also let your employees know that you are watching where your money goes. After balancing my register and filling out this sheet, I take all the receipts off the spindle and wrap them up with the cash register tape and any bank deposit slips I have. These little bundles are kept together until the end of the month, when each category is totaled and logged onto one sheet. From these sheets I do my monthly sales taxes, and from the 12 sheets accumulated over the year I can get the necessary information to do my income taxes. All the receipts for business expenses paid by cash are kept with these monthly bundles, while receipts for expenses paid by check are kept separately. You should have a separate checking account for your business, and if you need money from it for personal uses, a check can be written to deposit into your personal account. All receipts for anything paid with this account should be kept in a separate file folder. In this folder should also be the state sales tax worksheet used to compute the sales tax you pay the state.

Employee Taxes

I will not attempt to explain the minefield of laws, rules, and regulations that surrounds employing someone. I use tax tables provided by my accountant to figure out what I should withhold from my employees' checks. I turn these figures over to him every quarter, and he takes it from there. He fills out the necessary forms, and I sign them and pay what I must. You will need a good accountant. Find one and stick with him. Get his advice on how to keep records, when to pay taxes, and how to keep your books.

9 Conclusion

It is my sincerest hope that you will be able to use my knowledge of pawnbroking to become a successful pawnbroker. I also hope that I have not made it sound too easy. It is hard work to build a successful pawnshop from scratch. There are many things about this business that can be learned only by doing them. If you make a mistake, learn from it, and don't repeat it. You may also discover, if this is your first attempt at self employment, that you will work twice as hard for yourself as you did for someone else. When I first opened my shop, I sometimes put in 80-hour weeks. It took many years before I was able to pay myself anything but pocket change, because I reinvested every dime of profit back into my business. If my wife had not been well employed with good benefits, I would have had a hard time making ends meet. I recommend that you not plan on making a decent living from your business for about two years.

Honesty is an absolute must to be successful in the pawnshop business. Opportunities will present themselves every day to test your honesty. People will try to talk you into all manner of dishonest and illegal deals. You may get away with a lot before you are caught, but getting caught can flush all your hard work and sacrifice down the drain. My father had his license threatened once because of some dishonest actions by some of his employees. It's hard enough to keep from breaking laws unintentionally, let alone breaking them knowingly. The best policy is to follow all the laws to the best of your ability and pay the taxes that you are required to pay. Cheaters never prosper.

Finally, pawnbroking is a people business. You need people to pawn things, sell things, and buy things. You need regular customers who come and see you when they have a financial shortfall or when they have a financial windfall to spend in your store. You must be good with people and good to people. Don't get me wrong; you don't have to put up with any crap from jerks. The customer is not always right. You pay the rent in your store, and you should have everything your way. All most people want is a fair shake and a good deal. If you treat people with respect, then you have the right to get respect from them in return. I try to build up my base of good customers and weed out the buttheads. The more happy customers you have, the more success you will achieve. Good luck.

A Virginia Laws Governing Pawnbrokers

The following text is from the Virginia Code Commission's Code of Virginia (vol. 7A[1950]. sec. 54.1-4000–4014). It covers the state regulations by which pawnbrokers must conduct their business in Virginia. You should obtain copies of all the state laws governing pawnshops in the state where you intend to do business. You can find a complete set of state law books in your local library.

§ 54.1-4000   PROFESSIONS AND OCCUPATIONS   § 54.1-4001

Cross references. — As to punishment for Class 1 misdemeanors, see § 18.2-11.

Law Review. — For survey of Virginia law on business associations for the year 1974-1975, see 61 Va. L. Rev. 1650 (1975).

SUBTITLE V.
OCCUPATIONS REGULATED BY LOCAL GOVERNING BODIES.

CHAPTER 40.
PAWNBROKERS.

§ 54.1-4000. Definition of pawnbroker. — "Pawnbroker" means any person who lends or advances money or other things for profit on the pledge and possession of personal property, or other valuable things, other than securities or written or printed evidences of indebtedness, or who deals in the purchasing of personal property or other valuable things on condition of selling the same back to the seller at a stipulated price. (Code 1950, § 54-840; 1988, c. 765.)

§ 54.1-4001. License authorized by court; building designated in license; penalty. — The circuit court of any county or city may authorize any county, city or town to issue to any individual who produces satisfactory evidence of his good character, a license to engage in the business of a pawnbroker in that county, city or town. No such license shall be issued by any county, city or town except with such authority. Prior to the issuance of the license, the applicant shall furnish his date of birth and such other information to the licensing authority as may be required by the governing body. The license shall designate the building in which the licensee shall carry on such business. No person shall engage in the business of a pawnbroker without being licensed.

No person shall engage in the business of a pawnbroker in any location other than the one designated in his license, except with consent of the court which authorized the license. Any person who violates the provisions of this section shall be guilty of a Class 4 misdemeanor. Each day's violation shall constitute a separate offense. (Code 1950, §§ 54-841, 54-842; 1982, c. 633; 1986, c. 316; 1988, c. 765.)

Cross references. — As to punishment for Class 4 misdemeanors, see § 18.2-11.

This section and former § 54-842 do not expressly or by implication undertake to oust municipalities from imposing further restrictions upon the grant of the license. On the contrary, § 54.1-4002 contemplates and expressly authorizes further legislation. Additional reasonable conditions or restrictions not in conflict with the statute are not prohibited.

§ 54.1-4002   CODE OF VIRGINIA   § 54.1-4006

Flax v. City of Richmond, 189 Va. 273, 52
S.E.2d 250 (1949) (decided under prior law).

§ 54.1-4002. Local limitations as to number of pawnshops. — In
addition to all limitations and restrictions and notwithstanding any other
relevant provisions of this chapter, the governing body of any county, city or
town may limit by resolution or ordinance the number of pawnshops that may
be operated at any one time within its territorial limits.

The circuit court of any county or city which has, by resolution or ordinance,
limited the number of pawnshops therein shall not authorize any license to
any pawnbroker after the commissioner of the revenue or other tax assessing
officer of the county, city or town over which it has jurisdiction for the
issuance of such licenses has filed with the court a statement that the number
of licensed pawnshops within the county, city or town has reached the
maximum number of pawnshops authorized to be operated therein, unless the
number has been reduced below the maximum prescribed. (Code 1950,
§ 54-843; 1982, c. 633; 1988, c. 765.)

Constitutionality. — This section does not
undertake to give arbitrary power or delegate
legislative authority. It is constitutional and
does not violate the equal rights clause of the
state or federal Constitution. Flax v. City of
Richmond, 189 Va. 273, 52 S.E.2d 250 (1949)
(decided under prior law).
The grant of exclusive privileges to limited numbers and even to one person or
corporation, when justified under the police
power, does not fall within the ban of what is
termed a trust, combination or monopoly under
state or federal law. Flax v. City of Richmond,
189 Va. 273, 52 S.E.2d 250 (1949) (decided
under prior law).

§ 54.1-4003. Private action on bond. — Any person who recovers a
judgment against a licensed pawnbroker for the pawnbroker's misconduct
may maintain an action in his own name upon the bond of the pawnbroker if
the execution issued upon such judgment is wholly or partially unsatisfied.
(Code 1950, § 54-845; 1988, c. 765.)

§ 54.1-4004. Memorandum to be given pledgor. — Every pawnbroker
shall at the time of each loan deliver to the person pawning or pledging
anything, a memorandum or note, signed by him, containing the information
required by § 54.1-4009. A one-time two dollar service fee may be charged for
any such entry, memorandum or note. (Code 1950, § 54-846; 1968, c. 438;
1983, c. 238; 1988, c. 765.)

§ 54.1-4005. Sale of goods pawned. — No pawnbroker shall sell any
pawn or pledge until (i) it has been in his possession for four months, unless a
shorter period of not less than thirty days is agreed to in writing by the
pawner, and (ii) a statement of ownership is obtained from the pawner. All
sales of items pursuant to this section shall be made at a public auction
conducted by a licensed auctioneer. The governing body of the locality
wherein the pawnbroker conducts his business may determine the contents of
the statement of ownership. (Code 1950, § 54-847; 1986, c. 316; 1988, c. 765.)

§ 54.1-4006. Notice of sale. — Notice of every sale of a pawn or pledge
shall be published for at least five days prior to the sale in one or more daily
newspapers of general circulation in the county or city in which the
pawnbroker does business. The notice shall specify the time and place of the
sale, the name of the auctioneer, the kinds of articles to be sold and the
number of the pawner's ticket. (Code 1950, § 54-848; 1988, c. 765.)

§ 54.1-4007   PROFESSIONS AND OCCUPATIONS   § 54.1-4009

§ 54.1-4007. Disposition of surplus. — After deductions are made for the amount of the loan, interest due on the loan and the expenses of advertising and conducting the sale, the pawnbroker shall pay any money remaining from the proceeds of the sale to the person who would have been entitled to redeem the pledge if the sale had not taken place. (Code 1950, § 54-849; 1988, c. 765.)

§ 54.1-4008. Interest chargeable. — No pawnbroker shall ask, demand or receive a greater rate of interest than ten percent per month on a loan of $25 or less, or seven percent per month on a loan of more than $25 and less than $100, or five percent per month on a loan of $100 or more, secured by a pledge of tangible personal property. No loan shall be divided for the purpose of increasing the percentage to be paid the pawnbroker. (Code 1950, § 54-850; 1983, c. 238; 1988, c. 765.)

§ 54.1-4009. Records to be kept; credentials of person pawning goods. — A. Every pawnbroker shall keep at his place of business an accurate and legible record of each loan or transaction in the course of his business. The account shall be recorded at the time of the loan or transaction and shall include:
  1. A description, serial number, and a statement of ownership of the goods, article or thing pawned or pledged or received on account of money loaned thereon;
  2. The time, date and place of the transaction;
  3. The amount of money loaned thereon at the time of pledging the same;
  4. The rate of interest to be paid on such loan;
  5. The full name, residence address, work place, and home and work telephone numbers of the person pawning or pledging the goods, article or thing, together with a particular description, including the height, weight, date of birth, race, gender, hair and eye color, and any other identifying marks, of such person;
  6. Verification of the identification by the exhibition of a government-issued identification card such as a driver's license or military identification card. The record shall contain the type of identification exhibited, the issuing agency, and the number thereon;
  7. The terms and conditions of the loan, including the period for which any such loan may be made; and
  8. All other facts and circumstances respecting such loan.
  B. The Superintendent of State Police shall promulgate regulations specifying the nature of the particular description for the purposes of subdivision A 5 above.
  The Superintendent of State Police shall promulgate regulations specifying the nature of identifying credentials of the person pawning or pledging the goods. Such credentials shall be examined by the pawnbroker, and an appropriate record retained thereof. (Code 1950, § 54-851; 1976, c. 66; 1986, c. 316; 1988, c. 765; 1990, c. 783.)

The **1990 amendment,** in subsection A, inserted "serial number" in subdivision 1, substituted "The time, date and place of the transaction" for "The time of receiving the same" in subdivision 2, in subdivision 5, inserted "full," deleted "and" following "name," inserted "address, work place, and home and work telephone numbers," and inserted the language beginning "including the height" and ending "any other identifying marks," added subdivision 6, and redesignated former subdivisions 6 and 7 as present subdivisions 7 and 8.

§ 54.1-4010   CODE OF VIRGINIA   § 54.1-4014

§ 54.1-4010. Daily reports. — Every pawnbroker shall prepare a daily report of all goods, articles or things pawned or pledged with him that day and file such report by noon of the following day with the chief of police or other law-enforcement officer of the county, city or town where his business is conducted designated by the local attorney for the Commonwealth to receive it. The report shall include the name and residence of the pledgor and a description of the goods, article or thing pledged and shall be in writing and clearly legible to any person inspecting it.

Any person, firm or corporation violating any of the provisions of this section shall be guilty of a Class 4 misdemeanor. (Code 1950, § 54-853; 1988, c. 765.)

Cross references. — As to punishment for Class 4 misdemeanors, see § 18.2-11.

§ 54.1-4011. Officers may examine records or property; warrantless search and seizure authorized. — Every pawnbroker and every employee of the pawnbroker shall admit to the pawnbroker's place of business during regular business hours, the chief law-enforcement officer, or his designee, of the jurisdiction where the business is being conducted, or any law-enforcement official of the state or federal government. The pawnbroker or employee shall permit the officer to (i) examine all records required by this chapter and any article listed in a record which is believed by the officer to be missing or stolen and (ii) search for and take into possession any article known to him to be missing, or known or believed by him to have been stolen. (Code 1950, §§ 54-852, 54-854; 1988, c. 765; 1990, c. 683.)

The 1990 amendment rewrote this section.

§ 54.1-4012. Property pawned not to be disfigured, changed or concealed. — No property received on deposit or pledge by any pawnbroker shall be disfigured or its identity destroyed or affected in any manner so long as it continues in pawn or in the possession of the pawnbroker, nor shall any property be concealed for forty-eight hours after the property is received by the pawnbroker. (Code 1950, § 54-855; 1988, c. 765.)

§ 54.1-4013. Care of blankets, clothing, etc. — Pawnbrokers shall store, or take care to protect from damage during disuse, all blankets, clothing, carpets, furs, rugs, dress goods, cloths, mirrors, oil paintings, glass and chinaware, pianos, organs, curtains, beddings and upholstered furniture pawned or pledged with them. Pawnbrokers shall be allowed to charge two percent per month in addition to the regular charges for the first three months, or part thereof, while such goods remain as pledge for money advanced. (Code 1950, § 54-856; 1988, c. 765.)

§ 54.1-4014. Penalty for violation by licensed pawnbroker. — Any licensed pawnbroker who violates any of the provisions of this chapter shall be guilty of a Class 4 misdemeanor. In addition, the court may revoke or suspend the pawnbroker's license for second and subsequent offenses. (Code 1950, §§ 54-857, 54-858; 1988, c. 765.)

Cross references. — As to punishment for Class 4 misdemeanors, see § 18.2-11.

B Pawnbroker's Sources and Services

Books

Schwed, Peter. *God Bless Pawnbrokers*. New York: Dodd, Mead and Co., 1975.

Simpson, William R. and Florence K. Simpson with Charles Samuels. *Hock Shop*. New York: Random House, Inc., 1954.

Computer Software for Pawnbrokers

BRJ Corp.
4322 Central Ave.
Albuquerque, NM 87108

Data Age Business Systems
5281 Park St. N.
St. Petersburg, FL 33709

Ideal Software Systems, Inc.
P.O. Box 2928
Meridian, MS 39302

JMT Company
P.O. Box 546
Statesville, NC 28677-0546

Munz Computer Services
2201 N. Loop 35
Suite C
Alvin, TX 77511

Pawn Power, Inc.
740 N.E. 120th St.
Miami, FL 33161

Pawndex-Teknon Inc.
2932 N.W. 122
Suite 24
Oklahoma City, OK 73120

Sound Logic, Inc.
800 S. Pacific Coast Hwy.
Suite 8196
Redondo Beach, CA 90277
(loan arranger)

Vertical Computer Systems
3201 W. Commercial Blvd.
Suite 127
Ft. Lauderdale, FL 33309

Computerized Trading Networks

Pawnbroker's Net
21 Charles St.
Westport, CT 06880

Polygon Network, Inc.
P.O. Box 4806
Dillon, CO 80435-4806

Insurance

TWT Associates, Inc.
Rosemary Chacon-Cain
2524 E. Indian School Rd.
Phoenix, AZ 85016

Union Life and Casualty Agency
5225 N. Central
Suite 110
Phoenix, AZ 85012

Pawn Tickets

Burrell Printing Co., Inc.
P.O. Box 1340
Pflugerville, TX 78660

Pawnbroker Training Aids

United, Inc.
P.O. Box 18646
Charlotte, NC 28218

Pawnbroker's Associations and Publications

Jeweler's Circular and Keystone
Chilton Company
Chilton Way
Radnor, PA 19089
(monthly magazine)

National Pawnbroker's Association
P.O. Box 581368
Dallas, TX 75258

Pawn Bulletin
Impression Impact
113 Hill St.
Concord, MA 01742

Today's Pawnbroker magazine
150 Nassau St.
Suite 2030
New York, NY 10038

Photo ID Equipment and Supplies

ID Specialists, Inc.
2525 N.W. Expressway #513
Oklahoma City, OK 73112

Photoscope Corp.
320 W. Ohio St.
Chicago, IL 60610

Safes

Acme Safe Company
637 Lee St. S.W.
Atlanta, GA 30310

Empire Safe Co., Inc.
433 Canal St.
New York, NY 10013

Griffin Enterprises
140 Main St.
Chesterfield, SC 29709

Maximum Security Corp.
32841 Calle Perfecto
San Juan Capo, CA 92675

Statewide Safes and Vaults
851 S. Mollison
Unit 21
El Cajon, CA 92020

Worldwide Safe and Vault, Inc.
1746 N.W. 82nd Ave.
Miami, FL 33126

Storage Systems

Pipp Mobile Systems, Inc.
2862 Clydon S.W.
Grand Rapids, MI 49509

C · Jewelry Sources and Supplies

Appraisal Supplies and Instruments

File-A-Gem
120 W. 11th St.
Baxter Springs, KS 66713

Gemstone Press
P.O. Box 237
Woodstock, VT 05091

Appraisers

European Gemological Laboratory
550 S. Hill St.
Suite 1310
Los Angeles, CA 90013

Books

Hardy, R. Allen and John J. Bowman. *The Jewelry Repair Manual.* New York: Van Nostrand Rienhold Co., 1967.

Wycoff, Gerald. *Beyond the Glitter.* Washington, D.C.: Adamas Publishers, 1982.

Diamond Buyers

Bluestone Trading
P.O. Box 24126
Cleveland, OH 44124

Censor
15 W. 47th St.
Suite 1100
New York, NY 10036

Worldwide Diamond Co.
607 S. Hill St.
Los Angeles, CA 90014

Diamond Repair and Recutting

Chromagen
580 Fifth Ave.
New York, NY 10036

Schools

Bowman's Technical School
220 W. King St.
Lancaster, PA 17603

Dondor School of Fine Jewelry
8015-D Glenview Dr.
Fort Worth, TX 76180

Gemological Institute of America
1660 Stewart St.
Santa Monica, CA 90406

Holland Jewelry School
P.O. Box 882
Selma, AL 36702

Jeweler's Institute of America
P.O. Box 66
Statesboro, GA 30458

Jewelry Design Institute
P.O. Box 475
Sycamore Square
Midlothian, VA 23113

Jewelry Tech Institute
12831 Western Ave.
Suite H
Garden Grove, CA 92641

Louisville Jeweler's School
3206 Dupin Dr.
Louisville, KY 40219

Miami Jewelry Institute
Bakehouse Art Complex
561 N.W. 32nd St.
Miami, FL 33127

Revere Academy of Jewelry
760 Market St.
Suite 939K
San Francisco, CA 94102

Stewart's International School for Jewelers
651 Indiantown Rd.
Jupiter, FL 33458

Tampa Bay Jeweler's School
5305 Ehrlich Rd.
Tampa, FL 33625

Trenton Workshops
2505 Poplar Ave.
Memphis, TN 38112

Jewelry Buyers

C.M. Buxton Co.
105 S. Higgins
Missoula, MT 59802

Hafco
11 Grace Ave.
Suite 206
Great Neck, NY 11021

Jewel Cash, Inc.
62 W. 47th St.
Suite 211
New York, NY 11021

Jewelry Displays

Alsten Company
520 Palisades Ave.
Jersey City, NJ 07307

Gerald Fried Display Co., Inc.
550 Fillmore Ave.
Tonawanda, NY 14150

Noble
141 Lanza Ave.
Building 5
Garfield, NJ 07026

World Treasure, Inc.
2930 Merrell Rd.
Dallas, TX 75229

Jewelry Repair

Freeman's Jewelry Repair, Inc.
5840 S. Memorial Dr.
Suite 112
Tulsa, OK 74145

Jewelry Supplies

Archcrown, Inc.
280 Corporate Center
3 ADP Blvd.
Roseland, NJ 07068

B. Rush Apple
3855 W. Kennedy Blvd.
Tampa, FL 33609

C & M Enterprises
4111 S. Darlington
Suite 701
Tulsa, OK 74135

Cas-Ker Co.
2121 Spring Grove Ave.
P.O. Box 14069
Cincinnati, OH 45250-0069

Ed Mar
710 Samson St.
Philadelphia, PA 19106-3296

Kassoy
32 W. 47th St.
New York, NY 10036

Livesay's
456 W. Columbus Dr.
Tampa, FL 33602-1200

River Gems and Findings
6901 Washington N.E.
Albuquerque, NM 87109

Swest, Inc.
11090 North Stemmons Freeway
P.O. Box 59389
Dallas, TX 75229-1389

Jewelry, Wholesale

Bright Diamond International Corp.
25 W. 45th St.
New York, NY 10036

Eddie's Wholesale Jewelry Dist.
5641 Highway 90 W.
Theodore, AL 36582

The Frieden Company
P.O. Box 770420
Memphis, TN 38177-0420

Hafco
11 Grace Ave.
Suite 206
Great Neck, NY 11021

HMS Fine Jewelry
12770 Merit Dr.
Suite 122
Dallas, TX 75251

Italia International Jewelry, Inc.
999 Brannan St.
Suite 221
San Francisco, CA 94103

Jewels By Jack, Inc.
712 S. Olive St.
Suite 201-A
Los Angeles, CA 90014

Kim Imports, Inc.
14840 Landmark Blvd.
Suite 310
Dallas, TX 75240

Las Vegas Jewelry Company
3665 Las Vegas Blvd. S.
Las Vegas, NV 89109

Luke's Jewelry Company
60 Dalraida Rd.
Montgomery, AL 36109

Mid-Town Closeout
1083 S. State St.
Salt Lake City, UT 84111

Nation-Wide Jewelry
P.O. Box 6884
Hollywood, FL 33021

Olympia Gold
11540 Wiles Rd.
Suite 2
Coral Springs, FL 33076

Q.P.C. Jewelry, Inc.
1212 Avenue of the Americas
Suite 501
New York, NY 10036

Royal Chain, Inc.
2 W. 46th St.
New York, NY 10036

Savannah Gold Brokers
2302 Skidaway Rd.
Savannah, GA 31404

Superings, Inc.
411 W. 7th St. #801
Los Angeles, CA 90014

The Syeds Chimera, Inc.
7081 Grand National Dr.
Suite 109
Orlando, FL 32819

World Treasure, Inc.
2930 Merrell Rd.
Dallas, TX 75229

Refiners, Scrap Metal

Crystal Bay Trading
P.O. Box 123
Pomona, NY 10970

David H. Fell and Co., Inc.
6009 Bandini Blvd.
City of Commerce, CA 90040

Eastern Smelting and Refining Corp.
37-39 Bubier St.
Lynn, MA 01901

Garfield Refining Corp.
810 East Cayuga St.
Philadelphia, PA 19124

Houston Precious Metals
607 Chenevert
Houston, TX 77003

North American Metals
P.O. Box 8450
Van Nuys, CA 91409

Specialty Metals Refining Co.
10 Bay St.
Westport, CT 06880

Watch Buyers

Hess Fine Art
3637 4th St. N. #101
St. Petersburg, FL 33704

National Watch Exchange
107 S. 8th St.
Philadelphia, PA 19106

Specialty Metals
10 Bay St.
Westport, CT 06880

Watch Parts

Milano Imports, Inc.
P.O. Box 1732
Bellaire, TX 77402-1732
(Rolex)

Watch Repair

Dellani's
801 State St.
Santa Barbara, CA 93101

Max Katzenstein
285 Columbia Terr.
Paramus, NJ 07652

Pollack Watch Service, Inc.
13960 Cedar Rd.
Cleveland, OH 44118

Precision Crystal Cutting
23940 Eureka
Taylor, MI 48180

Sherman's Rolex Service
Box 22 Old Pattern Rd.
Island Falls, ME 04747

Watches, Wholesale

Esslinger and Co.
1165 Medallion Dr.
St. Paul, MN 55120

International Watchman
7670 Chippewa Rd.
Suite 418
Breckville, OH 44141

D Gun Sources and Supplies

Appraisal Guides

Blue Book Publications
One Appletree Square
Minneapolis, MN 55425

Flayderman's Guide to Antique American Firearms
by Norm Flayderman
D.B.I. Books, Inc.
4092 Commercial Ave.
Northbrook, IL 60062
(available at bookstores)

Orion Blue Book for Guns
Orion Research Corporation
1455 N. Scottsdale Rd.
Suite 330
Scottsdale, AZ 85254
(updated quarterly)

Bound Books for Gun Records

Hard Code Systems, Inc.
110 Bennett St.
Greenville, SC 29601
(computerized bound books)

NAFLFD American Firearms Industry Communications
Group, Inc.
2801 E. Oakland Park Blvd.
Fort Lauderdale, FL 33306

PFRB Company
P.O. Box 1242
Bloomington, IL 61701

Cases and Pouches for Guns

Ace Case Co.
1530 Pheasant Ridge
Ellisville, MO 63011

Brauer Brothers Manufacturing Co.
2020 Delmar
St. Louis, MO 63103

Firearms, Ammunition, and Supplies, Wholesale

Ashland Shooting Supplies
110 Baird Parkway
Mansfield, OH 44903

Interstate Arms Corp.
6-G Dunham Rd.
Billerica, MA 01821

Nationwide Sports Distributors, Inc.
RD 4, Box 369
Tyrone, PA 16686

RSR Wholesale Guns, Inc.
P.O. Box 60679
Rochester, NY 14606

Scott Wholesale Co., Inc.
P.O. Box 208
Indian Trail, NC 28079

Shotgun News
Snell Publishing Co.
P.O. Box 669
Hastings, NE 68902

Southern Ohio Gun
100 S. Mechanic St.
P.O. Box 590
Lebanon, OH 45036-0590

Firearms Parts and Accessories

The Gun Parts Corp.
Williams Lane W.
Hurley, NY 12491

Firearms Repair and Refinishing

Rebel Gun Refinishing
1203 S.W. 12th St.
Ocala, FL 32674

Publications

Shotgun News
Snell Publishing Co.
P.O. Box 669
Hastings, NE 68902

E ⋮ Other Merchandise Sources and Supplies

Appraisal Guides

Blue Book Publications
One Appletree Square
Minneapolis, MN 55425

Handbook of United States Coins
Western Publishing Co., Inc.
1220 Mound Ave.
Racine, WI 53404

Official Blackbook Price Guide
by Marc Hudgeons N.L.G.
The House of Collectibles
201 E. 50th St.
New York, NY 10022
(updated yearly)

Orion Blue Books for:
  · *Audio*
  · *Cameras*
  · *Car Stereos*
  · *Computers* (updated quarterly)
  · *Copiers*
  · *Guitars and Musical Instruments*
  · *Power Tools*
  · *Professional Sound*
  · *Video and TV*
  · *Vintage Guitars* (updated quarterly)
Orion Research Corporation
1455 N. Scottsdale Rd.
Suite 330
Scottsdale, AZ 85254
(updated yearly)

Archery Supplies

Archery Center International, Inc.
15610 S. Telegraph Rd.
Monroe, MI 48161

Kinsey's Archery Products, Inc.
1660 Steel Way Dr.
P.O. Box 100
Mount Joy, PA 17552-0100

Norman Archery Wholesale
8317 Gateway Terr.
Oklahoma, OK 73149

Binocular and Optic Repair Service

Greene-Carpenter Binocular Repair Service
205 Coventry Rd.
Virginia Beach, VA 23462

Camera Buyers

Charlotte Camera Brokers, Inc.
2400 Park Rd.
Charlotte, NC 28203

Columbus Camera Group, Inc.
55 E. Blake Ave.
Columbus, OH 43202

Coin Buyers

William S. Panitch, Inc.
855 Central Ave.
Suite 103
Albany, NY 12206

Coins

Littleton Coin Co.
253 Union St.
Littleton, NH 03561
(retail catalog)

Electronics, Wholesale

Factory Direct Marketing
12000 Merriman Rd.
Livonia, MI 48150

LES Distributors
Florida: 8888 N.W. 24th Terr.
             Miami, FL 33172
Indiana: P.O. Box 357
             Granger, IN 46530
Texas: 6025 Commerce Dr.
             Suite 545
             Irving, TX 75063

Ramko Distributing
34 S. Huron St.
Toledo, Ohio 43602

Santa Fe Distributing, Inc.
9640 Legler Rd.
Lanexa, KS 66219

The Wholesale House, Inc.
503 W. High St.
Hicksville, OH 43526

General Merchandise, Wholesale

M & M Merchandisers, Inc.
1923 Bomar Ave.
Fort Worth, TX 76103

Moore Sales Co.
11 Gilbert Rd.
Burkburnett, TX 76354

Guitar Buyers

Elderly Instruments
1100 N. Washington
P.O. Box 1421
Lansing, MI 48901

Gruhn Guitars
400 Broadway
Nashville, TN 37203

Knives

Blue Ridge Knives
Rt 6, Box 185
Marion, VA 24354-9351

Soque River Knives
P.O. Box 880
Clarksville, GA 30523

United Cutlery
1425 United Blvd.
Sevierville, TN 37862

Military Medals

Medals of America
1929 Fairview Rd.
Fountain Inn, SC 29644

Military Surplus, Wholesale

Flagler Surplus
1798 W. Flagler St.
Miami, FL 33135

Rothco
P.O. Box 986
Smithtown, NY 11787

Tarashinsky Merchandise Co.
256 Manhattan Ave.
Brooklyn, NY 11211

Musical Instrument Repair

Robert Frushour
Band Instrument Repair
15429 Motters Station Rd.
Rocky Ridge, MD 21778

Valley Repair Service
Band and Orchestra
9 N. Bruffey St.
Salem, VA 24153

Musical Instruments and Supplies, Retail

American Musical Supply
600 Industrial Ave.
Paramus, NJ 07652

Discount Music Supply
41 Vreeland Ave.
Totowa, NJ 07512-1120

Lark in the Morning
P.O. Box 1176
Mendocino, CA 95460

National Music Supply
P.O. Box 14421
St. Petersburg, FL 33733

Suncoast Music Distributing
P.O. Box 16965
St. Petersburg, FL 33733

Veneman Music
12401 Twinbrook Parkway
Rockville, MD 20852

Musical Instruments and Supplies, Wholesale

Advantage Wholesale Music Supply Co.
3359 N. Ridge Ave.
Arlington Heights, IL 60004

Davitt and Hanser
415 Greenwell Ave.
Cincinnati, OH 45238

E.M.M.C.
770-12 Grand Blvd.
Deer Park, NY 11729

Geneva International Corp.
29 East Hintz Rd.
Wheeling, IL 60090

International Music Co.
P.O. Box 2344
Fort Worth, TX 76113-2344

La Playa Distributing Co.
32059 Milton
Madison Heights, MI 48071

Martin Telemarketing
510 Sycamore St.
Nazareth, PA 18064

Musicorp
P.O. Box 30819
Charleston, SC 29417

Saga Musical Instruments
429 Littlefield Ave.
Box 2841
South San Francisco, CA 94080

V.J. Rendano Wholesale Music, Inc.
7152 Market St.
Boardman, OH 44512

Periodical

Close Out News
P.O. Box 8366
Holland, MI 49422-8366

Silverware Buyers

Atlantic Silver
7405 N.W. 57th St.
Tamarac, FL 33319

Beverly Bremer Silver Shop
3164 Peachtree Rd. N.E.
Atlanta, GA 30305

Walter Drake Silver Exchange
5000 Drake Bldg.
Colorado Springs, CO 80940

Sports Memorabilia Buyers

Central Pawn
Don Budd
100 Central
Kansas City, KS 66102

The Ring Man
P.O. Box 18194
Philadelphia, PA 19116

Steven Mitnick
29 Race St.
Frenchtown, NJ 08825

F ⋮ Business Sources

Advertising

Best Business Systems
6145 Barfield Rd.
Suite 110
Atlanta, GA 30328
(TV commercials for pawn shops)

Check Cashing

Check-Express
101 E. Kennedy Blvd.
Suite 3800
Tampa, FL 33602

Checklist magazine
150 Nassau St.
Suite 2030
New York, NY 10038

Chek-Mate
450 Main St.
Springfield, MA 01105

Electronic Tax Filing

Lightning Tax
P.O. Box 6
Provo, UT 84603

National Electronic Filing Co.
1107 S.W. Grady Way
Suite 202
Renton, WA 98055

Money Orders

Global Express Money Orders
P.O. Box 8608
Silver Springs, MD 20907